THE
MAKING OF AMERICA
SERIES

CARROLL COUNTY
A PLACE TO CALL HOME

This image shows the 1973 Carrollton Warrior Cheerleaders (left to right): Kathy Ocel, Wendy Guess, Kathy Bland, Peggy Peterson, and Vickie Mills. (Velma Griffin Collection.)

THE

MAKING OF AMERICA

SERIES

CARROLL COUNTY
A PLACE TO CALL HOME

JANICE E. LANE

ARCADIA
PUBLISHING

ISBN 978-0-7385-2422-1

Published by Arcadia Publishing
Charleston, South Carolina

Printed in the United States of America

Library of Congress Catalog Card Number: 2003100019

For all general information contact Arcadia Publishing at:
Telephone 843-853-2070
Fax 843-853-0044
E-Mail sales@arcadiapublishing.com
For customer service and orders:
Toll-Free 1-888-313-2665

Visit us on the Internet at www.arcadiapublishing.com

Front cover: *This image shows the train depot in Carrollton in 1913. This was the second depot built in Carrollton, which was replaced by the current depot now used by the Elderberry Excursion Line. (Courtesy Dr. and Mrs. George Rankin.)*

Contents

Acknowledgments 6
Introduction 7

1. It Began With a Trail 8
2. Taming the Land 19
3. The Canal Era and a New County 39
4. All Aboard! 53
5. Reading, Writing, and Arithmetic 73
6. One God, Many Faiths 93
7. The Civil War Years 116
8. The Turn of the Century 130
9. All Work and No Play . . . Never! 145
10. Here and Now 153

Bibliography 157
Index 159

Acknowledgments

When writing a history, it seems everyone has a story to tell and it's these stories that make our history interesting. Although it is not possible to list everyone I met on the street who contributed in some way, I do wish to thank them and especially the collections made available to me through the Genealogical Library. The works of the late Velma Griffin were the biggest source of information and I thank Donald Rutledge for permission to use her work and photo collections.

Without Dr. George and Helen Rankin, I would still be searching for answers to the mysteries of Carrollton and would not have found the vintage photos that cover this book. Thank you!

The facts and statistics were mainly from Carroll County auditor E. Leroy VanHorne, who is also my father and who has given me great support throughout this work. I thank him for instilling a love of history and genealogy in me that led to this work. I thank the rest of my family for their patience and help when called upon and my sister Amanda VanHorne especially for her photography talents.

It was through much cooperation and the patience of Genealogical Society president Jean Scarlott and Historical Society president Tom Konst that I was able to track down additional information and photos. They were quick to help me in any way they could. Thank you! I also thank Shirley Anderson, curator of the McCook House Museum, for helping look for the historical society photos.

One cannot forget Dick Griffin and Dan Rees for their photographs and postcards that complete this work. I also thank Karen Gray, Vickie Nign, Beth Johnston, and Tom Shearer for providing information on the schools.

Last but not least, I am so thankful for former residents, whom I was able to contact through the Internet, who also helped answer my questions and led me to photos, especially Sharen Shultz Bowers for her help with Leesville.

INTRODUCTION

In today's world, we worry about inner-city crime, school shootings, and terrorism. While Carroll County is not exempt from violence, being a place of small communities it is easy to forget about the problems of the world. You have probably heard the expression, "It's a nice place to visit, but I wouldn't want to live there." This statement does not fit Carroll County. Instead, it is the kind of place you go home to after being in those places. The increase in population over the past few years shows that more and more people are finding this to be true.

Some of the villages are now nothing more than a road sign, but remembrances of them will live forever in the residents, who will retell the legends and stories handed down for generations. Over the past 200 years, numerous people have trod upon the hills of Carroll County and called it home. Native Americans, Johnny Appleseed, the Daniel McCook family, and many others have helped create the legends and stories that will be told over and over again.

Not quite a Norman Rockwell painting, Carroll County's small-town charm and bustling activities offer more than one might think. There are no shopping malls or high-rise buildings; in fact, there are no cities. Yet, there is a comfort living in an area where nearly everyone knows your name. My husband often jokes that if you are not related to anyone when you first arrive, wait around long enough and you will be. This may not be completely true, but with the rich heritage here and the long list of forefathers, it may come close.

I regret that I cannot list every single person who has come through Carroll County, especially since I am sure many of you are reading this in hopes of finding a piece to your genealogical puzzle. With the space limit, I intend to focus on the historical highlights and those people who played significant roles in our heritage. Should those people connect to you, then I am glad I could help. For the rest of us, I hope I can lead you to the information that will locate those missing pieces. Overall, I hope to share with you what has made Carroll County what it is and give hope to those who will make the future stories and tell the legends of us to the generations to come.

1. It Began With a Trail

The early history of Carroll County may seem more like an American History lesson than a local one, but without this knowledge, it is hard to imagine how settlers found their way to this seemingly remote area. Situated in what is now mid-eastern Ohio, the land now known as Carroll County was once only a dense wilderness inhabited by Native Americans. We know this because of written records left by the French and English who explored, trapped, traded, or settled in Ohio during the 1600s and 1700s. No native tribes settled in the Ohio region until the early 1700s, but the land provided a great hunting ground for many groups. No one knows why natives did not settle in Ohio during this period, but it is likely that the strong Iroquois group from New York kept this region from being inhabited. The Iroquois were warlike people who fought with other tribes and drove them from their lands. Once the Europeans began pushing further west, natives had no choice but to begin settling the Ohio region.

The only tribe known to live entirely in Carroll County at that time was the Delaware. This tribe originally lived in what is now the state of Delaware and parts of Pennsylvania. They were known to be a peaceable tribe, but more hostile tribes called the Delaware "old women." The Delaware referred to themselves as Leni-Lenape, meaning "real men." The Delaware camp was located approximately 5 miles south of Carrollton and consisted of mostly wigwams and caves. The Iroquois were the next closest tribe, occupying the land north of Carroll County all the way to Lake Erie.

We know Native Americans were here from artifacts found throughout the area. In 1840, while digging for his cellar, earthenware coffins were found on Nathaniel Shaw's farm. Unfortunately, these remains were not preserved and no longer exist. Along Stallion Road, just south of Harmony Cemetery, a stone was found that measured 10 feet in diameter and had seven deep areas hollowed out. A farmer who owned the land also found a pestle; it is believed the stone was used to grind and cook corn. According to legend, the Native Americans would add heated stones to the corn once it was ground, which was how they cooked it.

On this same farm, a tomahawk was found, as well as several arrowheads. Arrowheads, tomahawks, and other implements have also been found on various farms throughout the county. Other large "artifacts" left by the Native Americans were the trails they created going from northeast to southwest, to and from the Great Lakes and the Ohio and Mississippi Rivers. Other tribes, who were headed further south and west due to the white men settling the east, passed through this part of the county on what is now called "The Great Trail." It was also known as the Tuscorara Path and was thought to be the great migration route to the west. This trail began in the state of Delaware, crossed through Pennsylvania to the Ohio River near Pittsburgh, and then entered Ohio just north of Lisbon. Leading west, it crossed the Little Beaver, proceeded southwest, crossed the Little Beaver again, and went on to Painted Post. The post marked the junction of the Great Trail with the Moravian Trail. From Painted Post, the Great Trail led west to Hanoverton, Kensington, and into the northernmost portion of Carroll County through Minerva, Pekin, Oneida, Malvern, Magnolia, and Sandyville before entering Tuscarawas County north of Fort Laurens. Then it went northwest to Beach City, Sugar Creek Flats, Mt. Eaton, Apple Creek Valley, and on to

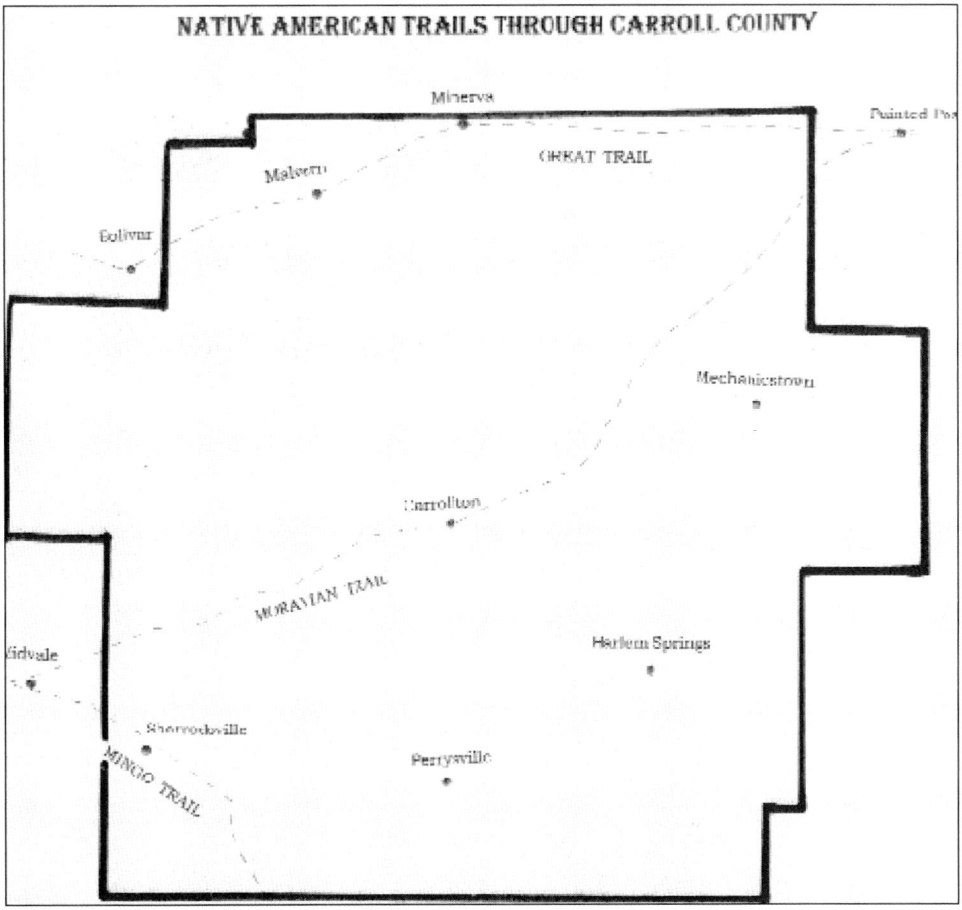

This map indicates where the Native American trails passed through Carroll County. A commemorative marker is in Malvern Park.

This woodcut by John Rae shows what John Chapman, better known as Johnny Appleseed, may have looked like.

another major trail north of Wooster, which follows State Route 250, crossing the Cuyahoga War Trail and proceeding northwest. The Great Trail then led to Fort Sandusky on Lake Erie and skirted the west end of Lake Erie to Fort Detroit. This trail was the main overland route between Fort Pitt and Fort Detroit.

These trails were vastly important in the settlement and development of Ohio. In many instances, they determined the location of white settlements, forts, and military roads, some of them later becoming public highways. Along these trails, the native tribes passed from one location to another, whether engaged in warfare, the chase, trade, or migration. Together with the navigable streams, the trails served as the means of entrance to the white traders and settlers who pushed their way into the country north and west of the Ohio River. The Great Trail was used extensively during the French and Indian War, Pontiac's Rebellion, the American Revolution, and the Ohio Indian Campaigns.

Another trail passed below Bergholz and ran through the southern portion of Carroll County along the Elkhorn Creek south of Harlem Springs. Although it has never been found, a legend claims the tribe who settled that area used to have mines of a very fine high-grade lead ore. Other tribes that are believed to have used these trails are the Ottawas, Shawnee, and Huron.

Yet another trail was the Moravian. A part of it proceeded with the Great Trail from Pennsylvania into Ohio before heading southwest at Painted Post through Carroll County to the Indian Fork of Conotton Creek. It crossed where Atwood Dam is today. From there, it passed over the Little Stillwater before heading west to just north of Dennison. The trail went southwest to Uhrichsville, coming just

6 miles south of Schoenbrunn and 3 miles north of Gnadenhutten, before ending at the Mingo Trail.

Most of these tribes spoke Algonquin, and prior to the sixteenth century, they inhabited the area east of the Mississippi River, including Ohio. One of the chiefs in the area was Captain Pipe. He was peaceable as long as he was not intoxicated, but when he was, he would boast of murdering and it was never known if he meant white men or other natives. It was most likely the Great Trail that was used by Captain Pipe when he led Moravian missionary Frederick Post to the banks of the Muskingum River (now the Tuscarawas River) to talk with his tribe. Although Pipe never converted to Christianity, he was friendly to the Moravian missionaries and supported peace between the natives and settlers. Frederick Post built a log cabin near the Indian Village and it is believed to be the first white man's house in Ohio. When Post returned a year later, he planted the first known garden. This settlement was called Schoenbrunn.

Around this time, more hostile tribes were being pushed from the east by the colonists and thus began pushing the Algonquin-speaking tribes from their area. A legend printed in *The Carroll Republican* in February 1887 tells of four men who encountered some of this hostility. The four were scouts sent out from Fort McHenry in Virginia (now Wheeling, West Virginia) to Fort McIntosh at the mouth of Big Beaver Creek. Since the frontier had been divided into "beats" to protect it from hostile native attacks, the group was sent out to check the beat in this area. The team consisted of Captain James Downing, Isaac Miller, John Cuppy, and James (or Jason) Foulks. (Another source says that Anthony Wayne was actually the leader, but he is not mentioned in the 1887 account.)

They left Fort McHenry and headed along Wheeling Creek to Short Creek, then to the Conotton Creek, near present-day New Rumley in Harrison County, Ohio. On the fourth day, they reached present-day New Hagerstown in Carroll County. The next morning, they continued north and reached the Indian Fork at what was then called the "Indian Camp," just west of present-day Dellroy. As they approached the camp, they discovered a weird, half-naked figure with long black hair streaming in the wind, no shoes, and a few tattered rags covering his body. He was shy, but not frightened. He turned out to be John Chapman, better known as Johnny Appleseed.

Known for planting apple trees throughout the Northwest Territory, Johnny was on friendly terms with both whites and natives, and he warned the four not to proceed north as Captain Pipe's tribe and a hostile tribe from north of the Big Sandy were on the war path. Ignoring Appleseed's warnings, the four continued north over Baxter's Ridge and down into Pipe's Creek Fork toward the Big Sandy. Only one day from their destination, they decided to camp just south of present-day Minerva. Miller shot a deer for their dinner. Realizing the noise he had made, Miller then decided to heed Appleseed's warnings. Downing ordered everyone to their posts. Miller was to grain the deerskin to repair their footgear, while Foulks prepared supper and Cuppy arranged a place for them to rest. Downing went on duty as sentinel.

Downing had just taken his position and was carefully surveying his surroundings when he saw a warrior rise out of the grass, attracted perhaps by the smoke of their campfire. Downing fired his rifle and the warrior fell. The scouts seized their firearms and ran, only to discover they were being stalked by a war party led by Chief Yellowstone. Downing called for a retreat after realizing the natives outnumbered them. He then called out, "Every man for himself!"

The four immediately scattered, each taking a different route. Foulks took the trail for the Beaver, while Cuppy took a middle route to the Muddy Fork. After Downing started running toward the Still Fork, Miller noticed he was covered with blood and ran to him. It turned out to be a nosebleed. Miller took his knife and cut Downing's shirt collar and necktie so he could breathe easier and parted with, "Jim, run for your life." He then remained alone as a decoy.

Miller played the part well. He pranced back and forth to draw the fire of the natives and he succeeded. His real objective was to gain time for his comrades and give them time to get a good start. The whole tribe rushed after Miller with hideous yells. He taunted them as long as he dared to, then bounded southward with the whole crew in tow. He reached the Little Fork River near its mouth and crossed, not knowing how he had done so, for when he reached the southern side, his feet were dry. To have jumped it was impossible as the creek was swollen to nearly 25 feet. How he got over was always a mystery to him.

Once on the other side, Miller turned to look and saw a native just entering the water. He drew up his rifle and fired. The native fell, but Miller never knew if he killed him. He continued running south until he reached the site where New Harrisburg now stands. The sun had set, so he took his course by the North Star, turned east, passed where Carrollton now stands, and struck the headwaters of Yellow Creek, 3 miles to the east. Running all night, he followed the stream to its mouth.

The settlers back at Fort McHenry were very anxious as not a word had been heard from the men since they left. It was the only thing thought or talked about in the settlement. Everyone knew that if the scouts were killed or even captured, their weak settlement would be in immediate danger. They would be inundated with a tribe of angry natives and their captivity or death was only a question of time. To their surprise, a canoe glided across the river and landed carrying Miller. One at least was safe. Miller could tell that he had saved his own life and perhaps his commander's, but of the others, only God knew their fate.

Then anxiety was relieved, for by some miracle, they all returned singly by three different routes. They were all received with open arms by rejoicing friends. How far the natives had followed them they never knew.

Others who were in the area were not so lucky when they encountered the natives. About 1789, a man by the last name of Swearingen was hunting for ginseng with some others along the Ohio River near present-day Steubenville when he became ill. Swearingen stayed behind in camp while the others went off to search. It is then believed a group of hostile natives raided the camp and took Swearingen as captive. When the others returned to camp, they discovered their

These rocks marked the site of the first white man's grave. They were accidentally removed by a farmer. (Velma Griffin Collection.)

companion was missing and followed the trail to present-day Carrollton. At the J.B. McCully Spring, they found Swearingen's scalped and beaten body. They buried him on top of the hill, just southeast of the spring, and his is believed to be the first white man's grave in Carroll County.

There is a legend that tells of another precious item being buried as men traveled through the area. In 1755, a group of 10 French soldiers, trying to escape from the British just before they destroyed Fort Duquesne, were traveling the Tuscarora Trail with 16 pack mules loaded with $25,000 in gold and silver. This money had been taken in raids on the British about the time of General Edward Braddock's defeat. Braddock and his men were noted to have lost a payroll in this same amount and it is quite possible this money was it. While following the Great Trail enroute to Detroit, the French soldiers passed through Painted Post and the present town of Dungannon when their scouts reported signs of a Native American ambush. Quickly, they buried the gold and silver, leaving several clues to identify the location: the four springs that formed a square where they had stopped, their shovels hidden under some fallen trees, a deer's head carved into another tree, and a stone wedged in the fork of yet another. A map was made so they could one day return for their treasure. According to the map, the spot was in the north quarter of section four in Augusta Township. All but one of the men were killed by the Native Americans and the survivor took the map and went south to North Carolina. Many years later, a man claiming to be a descendant of the survivor returned to tell this tale and search for the buried treasure. He and many others after him found the clues, but were never able to find the treasure.

A trend soon began wherein military forces used the trails. In 1764, Colonel Henry Bouquet used the Great Trail during the campaign to conquer the Pontiac and other rebellious tribes. Marching from Fort Pitt to the Tuscarawas-Muskingum Valley, Colonel Bouquet and his men camped near present-day Pekin before continuing toward Chillicothe. He was headed for present-day Goldcliff Park, which was then called the Lower Shawnee Town. They ended up in Coshocton, where he and his men freed 200 captives held by Chief Pontiac and his Ottawa tribe. After a show of force, a treaty was signed by Colonel Bouquet and the chiefs of the Seneca, Delaware, and Shawnee tribes. This treaty helped break Pontiac's Conspiracy and did much to open the "Ohio Country."

Then, in 1778, another group of soldiers passed through. Ordered by General George Washington, General Lachlan McIntosh was sent to build a fort in Ohio to serve as a protection for the exposed portion of the frontier from Native American attacks, and to provide a base for a spring campaign on Fort Detroit, which was held by the British and allied tribes. Setting out from Fort Pitt, McIntosh and an army of 1,200 men followed the Great Trail into Ohio. Along the way weather worsened, and on the nights of November 13 and 14, 1778, the expedition camped on what is now Malvern Park. They joined forces with friendly Delaware and proceeded to the Tuscarawas River, where they succeeded in building Fort Laurens.

McIntosh and his men camped in what is now Malvern Park. This marker commemorates his visit.

By the end of the Revolutionary War, colonists were pushing their way westward to the banks of the Ohio River and they began using the trails to find new homes. Since the new government had no money to pay its soldiers, but had lots of land, it used the land to pay the soldiers by issuing each a warrant for a certain number of acres in the western territory. Each warrant differed according to a man's rank and length of service. If the soldier died in the war, his family received the warrant for his land. These warrants were usually for areas from 100 to 15,000 acres. Describing the specific pieces of land was not easy and the boundaries were unclear because there was not a consistent method of marking the tracts of land.

Seeking a plan to solve this problem and carve new states in the vast new territory, Thomas Jefferson proposed the idea of surveying the land into tracts. His proposal was modified through the legislative process and eventually turned into the Land Ordinance of 1785. This recommended that the land be marked in areas shaped like squares. Since the Earth's surface is round and not flat, the parcels were not perfectly square, but were close.

The Delaware, Shawnee, Miami, Mingo, and Mohican tribes, all Algonquin speaking, who inhabited the area north and west of the Ohio River, formed a federation against this. They had hoped the land they occupied, particularly the new state of Ohio and much of the Northwest Territory, would become an Indian State, the 14th, subject to the same laws as the original 13. Supposedly, the Congressional Act of 1787 had ceded this land to them forever; in actuality, all it did was lay out the laws for governing the Northwest Territory, encouraging the platters and homesteaders to move in.

Thomas Jefferson's plan required that all public lands be divided into townships 6 miles square. Each township would be divided into 36 sections, each 1 mile by 1 mile square, equal to 640 acres. Then each section was divided into 160-acre quarters that could be broken down further into farms or town lots. The townships were laid out east to west and north to south of right angle base lines. The east and west line was known as the geographer's line. Every 6 miles was a township corner and lines were run south to the Ohio River from these corners. Townships between any two of these lines were designated as a range. A range is a vertical row of townships, with each being 6 miles by 6 miles square. They were then numbered, starting in the lower right-hand corner and moving north. The first surveyed land was called the Seven Ranges because it was seven ranges west of the point where the Ohio River meets the western boundary of Pennsylvania. Basically, the Seven Ranges are the eastern boundary of Ohio. This tract of land was the very first to use the federal survey system under the Public Land Act of 1785. Today, 29 states require a legal description of a parcel of land for sale. This description contains the numbers of the range, township, section, and part of the section with the original survey name.

At the corners of Stark, Tuscarawas, and Carroll Counties stands an original granite marker about 12 inches high and 6 inches across. It is exactly 42 miles due west of the beginning point for surveying the public lands of the United States and marked the terminus of the seventh range of townships surveyed in the Northwest Territory in 1786. It marked the completion of the first phase of the United States Public Land Survey. From this stone, the survey extended south for about 84 miles, reaching the Ohio River just a few miles above Marietta. This stone is also important in that it marked the western terminus of the geographer's line of the Seven Ranges and the eastern terminus of the Greeneville, or General Anthony Wayne's Treaty Line of 1795.

Under the leadership of Miami chief "Little Turtle," the Native Americans decided to make a stand for their lands. This resulted in three bloody massacres. Around the same time, the missionaries stationed in the area asked for protection against hostile Native Americans. George Washington turned to General Wayne, who was sent with a group of soldiers. These troops crossed the southern portion of Carroll County and camped in Loudon Township. Today, this area is near the intersection of Post and Profit Roads along Irish Creek, just 2 miles south of present-day Kilgore. Little Turtle felt he could not be surprised and should be negotiated with, while the other natives felt he was softening. The natives proceeded to fight the militia. General Wayne defeated them at the Battle of Fallen Timbers and the Greeneville Treaty was signed. The treaty line went all the way across Ohio into Indiana and then south to the Kentucky line. By signing this treaty, the Native Americans were pushed from Ohio and dispossessed of all their lands east of the Mississippi River. In grief, terrible sickness, and poverty, they crossed the Mississippi to the west. Only a handful remained behind. Captain Pipe, some of his tribe, and a one-legged native called Kan-nat-ten (Algonquin for one-leg) stayed. Kan-nat-ten remained because travel with the rest of his tribe would have been too difficult. The area he occupied was later named for him.

Our best knowledge of where the Great Trail was is due to a map drawn by Colonel Thomas Hutchins, who created it from his own surveys. It is his mark and plumb hole on the surveyor's stone. Colonel Hutchins, as the first geographer and surveyor general of the United States, conducted the first survey. He established the rectangular survey system that was specified "for ascertaining the mode of disposing lands in the western territory." The rectangular system was used to survey millions of acres, making up 31 states. By September 1786, Hutchins had surveyed 4 miles of base line and his men had completed four ranges. Surveying of the Seven Ranges was finished in July 1788.

After the first four ranges had been surveyed, Congress was concerned that the land was not selling, because the government needed the money for the national treasury. Since most of the land in the Ohio area still belonged to the federal government, it needed a way to sell the land. William Henry Harrison was serving as secretary to the Northwest Territory and had been elected as an 1800 delegate to Congress. He suggested that the government open land offices, which could sell land to the average person. Congress accepted his plan and it was called the Harrison Land Act or the Act of May 10, 1800. These offices were established in Steubenville, Cincinnati, Chillicothe, and Marietta. The first was officially opened in July 1800 in Steubenville. In 1808, a land office was opened in Canton.

The land in the Seven Ranges was offered in tracts of 640 acres for $1,280, or $2 per acre. This was considered too high for heavily forested land, so the minimum was reduced to a half section of 320 acres. The land still did not sell. Then, the land in the "Symmes Purchase" sold for 67¢ per acre and the land in the Seven Ranges began to sell once the minimum was reduced to a quarter section at $1.25 per acre. (Today, Carroll County's land averages $2,500 to $3,500 per acre.)

In 1786, what now makes up the state of Ohio was formed by an Act of Congress, and in the following year, a colony of emigrants from Massachusetts under the name of the New England Ohio Company came to what is now Marietta. In 1788, the first permanent settlement arose in the state. Arthur St. Clair, former president of the United States Assembly Congress, became governor of the area. The first county was formed after a proclamation by Governor St. Clair on

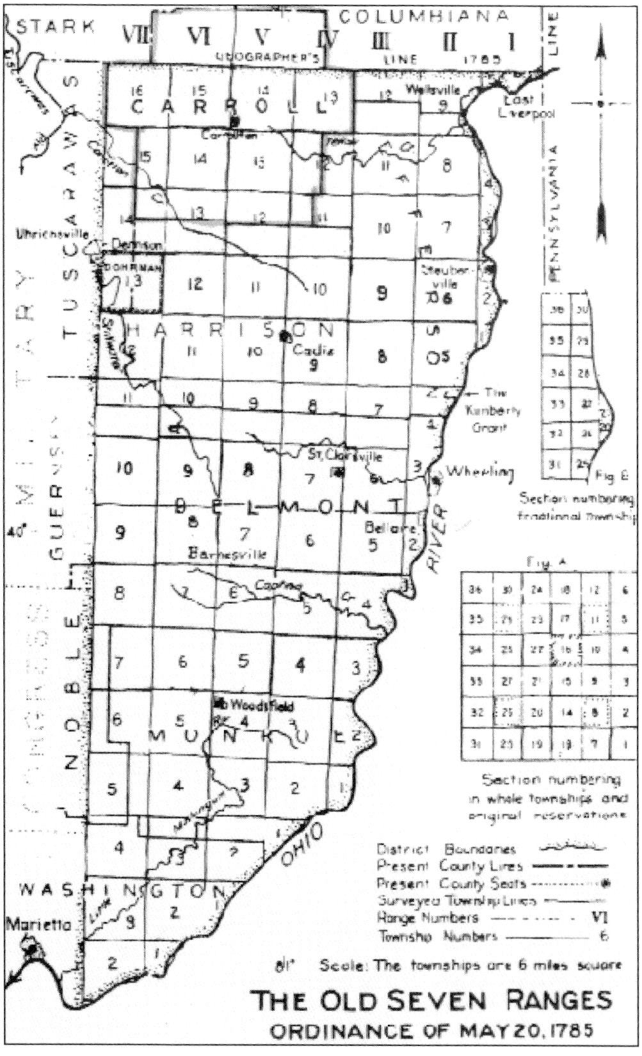

*This map shows the Seven Ranges as they were laid out in 1785. (*Centennial Edition.*)*

July 26, 1788. Marietta was chosen as its seat. The county, called Washington, extended northward to Lake Erie and westward to the Tuscarawas and Scioto Rivers. Slowly, other townships formed in this same area as more settlers moved in. The fifth township formed in the state was Jefferson County. Named for Thomas Jefferson, it was created on July 29, 1797 by proclamation of Governor St. Clair. The original boundaries included the country west of Pennsylvania and Ohio, and east and north of a line from the mouth of the Cuyahoga River, south to the Muskingum River, and east to the Ohio River. That same year, Bezaleel Wells established Steubenville and it became the county seat where the land office opened in 1804.

In 1803, when the federal requirement of 60,000 free adult males was met, Ohio became the first state admitted from the Northwest Territory. That same year, on March 25, a portion of Washington County and a portion of Jefferson were taken and another county was formed. Named for Christopher Columbus and Queen Anna, it was called Columbiana. By an act of the Ohio State Legislature on February 13, 1808, Stark County was drawn from land in Columbiana County. It was organized on January 1, 1809. Prior to 1815, Stark County had eight townships; one of those was Sandy Township, which organized March 16, 1809. Just two days after the act to form Stark County, on February 15, 1808, a portion of Muskingum County was taken to form Tuscarawas County. Then, on January 1, 1814, portions of Jefferson and Tuscarawas Counties were taken to form the county of Harrison. It was in the junction of these counties that our story begins.

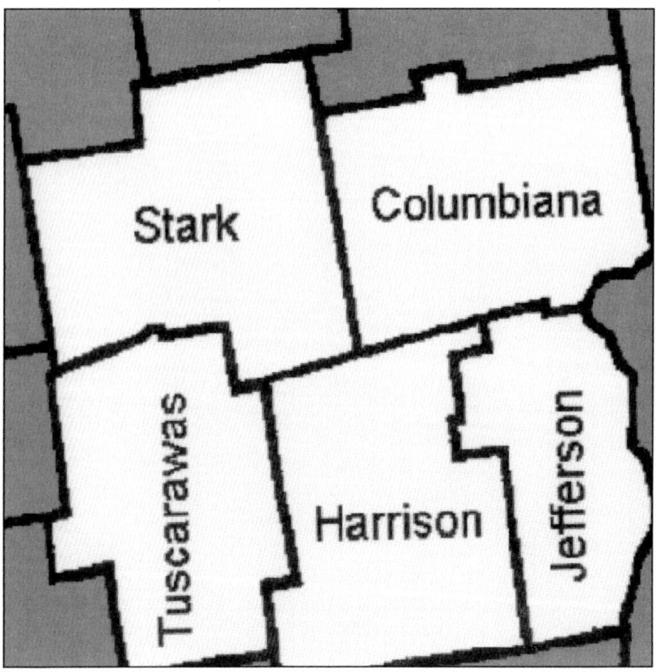

This 1814 map shows the boundary lines before Carroll County was taken from the five counties.

2. Taming the Land

Once the Ohio land was opened to settlers, they flooded in using whatever means possible. Often, the men would come alone to scope out the land and choose their claim, then build a small lean-to shelter. Many times, they chose land near a river or stream so they would have a convenient water supply. Upon establishing a dwelling, they would return to their former homes for their families. As mentioned earlier, the land was payment for service in the Revolutionary War, but not all pioneers were Revolutionary War veterans. Some came from Europe to escape poverty and hardship. Others, like the Germans and Quakers from Pennsylvania and the old families of Maryland, Kentucky, and Virginia, were attracted by the fertility of the soil and a chance to better their condition. (Western Pennsylvania and Kentucky were part of Virginia until the 1790s.)

The early settlers were all comparatively poor in worldly goods and had many contentions to face. Few people living today would have the courage to handle the hardships connected with carving a new world out of a wilderness in an alien land, where death and disease were constant companions, thanks to the constant threat of epidemics such as cholera, small pox, diphtheria, and scarlet fever. Without the antibiotics of today, these diseases wiped out entire families. The natives had found ways to use roots, plants, and tree bark to make medicine to heal their wounds and sicknesses, but the diseases of the white men were often too much.

By this time, the natives were no longer a problem for the settlers. The remaining Native Americans were actually very helpful. As stated earlier, Captain Pipe was only a problem if he had been drinking, but in 1811, he disappeared. It is believed he was murdered. Human bones were found, along with a gun barrel, on the banks of Pipe's Run Creek and no identification could ever be made.

Daniel Shambaugh, who was traveling through Carroll County from Harrison County, encountered a tribe of natives. He was going to enter a 640-acre section of land at the Canton Land office. The land cost $1 an acre and Shambaugh had to carry the money with him. At Indian Rocks, he met Chief White Eyes. When Shambaugh told him where he was going and why, Chief White Eyes took him into his buffalo skin wigwam and sat in the doorway all night with his bow and arrow, keeping watch while Shambaugh slept. The next morning, Shambaugh continued on to Canton and bought his land.

This photo of the Long family shows how many early settlers entered the Carroll County area. (Velma Griffin Collection.)

Chief White Eyes was known for this kindly behavior. His people traded with the settlers who were kind to them. His son, White Eyes Jr., succeeded him after his death, but unlike his father, he was lazy and did not provide for the tribe the way his father had. Chief White Eyes Jr. was known to have traded skins and other articles for whiskey instead of food and became quite a drunkard. As a result, most of the tribe then died from lack of food and from disease. This was the last tribe in Carroll County. Presumably, the others left when the treaties were signed ordering them to leave the Ohio territory.

The wild animals were often too much for the settlers. Their livestock was often attacked by bears, wolves, and wildcats. In later years, a Mr. Clark of Centrevile (now Carrollton) armed himself with a flint-lock musket and killed a bear on his property behind the Presbyterian Church (on North Lisbon and Second Street Southeast) and roasted the meat near the spring in the rear of Stockon's bank (where the Bureau of Support is today). The bear is not as abundant as it once was, but as late as 2001, a black bear was seen roaming through Carroll County in the Atwood area.

Wolves still live in the area, but are no longer the nuisance they once were. Most are kept as pets, but at one time, settlers were paid up to $12 by the authorities for the pelts. To keep wolves away, the knots of wood from pine would be placed around the cabin and set afire. They burned longer than a regular fire, and the light and smoke would keep the wolves at bay. A man named Valentine Friday would often tell of this practice, but admitted that, eventually, it did not keep them away. Apparently, the wolves realized there was no real danger.

Snakes, especially copperheads and rattlesnakes, were another problem and were extremely plentiful. The natives believed that the raccoons in the winter changed into snakes in the summer. Rattlesnakes were so plentiful that 12 to 15 of them could be killed in a single day. Soon after the Dellroy area was settled, a young girl was caring for an ill neighbor. While sitting on the porch churning butter, she heard a peculiar noise. Every time she stopped churning, the noise stopped. The woman she was caring for recognized the noise and sent the young girl for her husband. He lifted a floor board on the porch and found a rattlesnake ready to strike. He shot the snake and it is believed to have been the last one in the area.

According to the diary of a Schoenbrunn missionary, large herds of buffalo, deer, and other wild game roamed the area. Although the wildlife often caused problems for the settlers, they were also a great source of furs and meat. As food was difficult to obtain, they were thankful for the wild game. Johnny Appleseed also provided plenty of apples to accompany the meat. Johnny walked over most of western Pennsylvania and eastern Ohio year after year and would find a place along the road or at the edge of a woods, a place with plenty of moisture, and would plant a number of appleseeds. With his exceptional memory, he would remember these places and return years later to tend to the small orchard that had grown. (The last of his orchards in Carroll County was cleared in the 1970s.) Thus, many apple trees, especially in eastern Ohio, owed their origin to this man. Along with these apples, wild berries were another source of free and abundant food. Sometimes, if a settler happened to be near enough a stream, fish would be caught.

Their style of living was very primitive. There was so much to be done that settlers did little outside of daily toil. Their first few years in the new land were the most difficult. It is nearly unbelievable what they accomplished with the simple tools and equipment they had. Clearing the forest for crops so the settlers could produce clothing, food, and shelter was a struggle. In July 1800, some settlers were helped in this process by a tornado. Referred to as the Storm of Fallen Timbers, it cleared a path a half-mile wide and leveled practically every tree in its path, making it easier to clear the land for farms.

With a few tools and much labor, settlers began making what they needed, their first of which was shelter. A day or two would be taken by all of the men in the area to cut down the the tallest and straightest trees they could find. The timbers would be put into place, one by one, and carefully fitted at the corners to make the walls straight and solid. These cabins usually ranged in size from 15 to 25 feet square and were rarely over 10 feet high in the center. Even at this low height, many were a story and a half, the lower floor being around 6.5 to 7 feet high. If a man was taller than 6 feet, he would have to remove his hat to enter. The cracks between the logs were filled with short pieces of wood called "chinking" and these were daubed over with soft mud. The roof was usually made from clapboards, wood split from the trees and held on by long poles fastened by wooden pins. These were covered with split shakes, cut 3 to 4 feet long, and as thin as they could be without splitting. The floor was made a lot like the roof, only the boards were just laid in place or the earth was left and tramped until it was smooth. The door would swing on heavy wooden hinges, fastened with a wooden latch. A string that could be pulled through the latch was their "doorknob." Many times, this string was left on the outside during the day and pulled in only at night.

Usually, three open spaces were left in the walls of the cabin: one for the door, one for a window, and the third for a fireplace. Glass was too expensive to have windows like today; instead, the opening was covered with greased paper or left open with a "door" of its own that could be opened for light. The fireplace usually had a chimney made of stones. Few, if any, nails were ever used as they were not readily available.

After their homes were built, the settlers turned to preparing their farms. With the land cleared, enough grain and seeds were planted to make food for the next year. Corn was dropped by hand and then covered with a hoe. Oats and wheat were broadcast by hand and cultivated. Once they were ready to harvest, the crops were cut with a sickle, raked, and bound by hand. The grain was then threshed out by hand and sometimes flailed on the floors of their cabins. Too many times, the wheat was of very poor quality and would spoil easily, mainly because of moisture or because other vegetation grew too close. The spoiled wheat would

A rare find, this two-story cabin was built in 1825 and is now part of the Algonquin Mill farm.

Originally a home in another part of the county, this cabin represents the home of early settlers and now resides at the Algonquin Mill.

not always be detected until it was baked into bread and eaten, making the settlers very ill. To avoid this, they turned to making cornbread, but considered it to be inferior to the wheat bread.

To keep harvested apples, potatoes, and other vegetation from spoiling, they were kept in caves or buried in the ground. Many apples and peaches were dried for longer preservation.

Those who had livestock would also build a barn. In much the same fashion as the log home, each log would be cut and notched, and when they had enough, neighbors would come and help raise the barn. Of course, neighbors of that day were usually miles apart, so the entire event was usually planned well in advance. The men would come and build the barn, while the women prepared heaps of food for all the workers. The food would consist of hog and hominy, possibly bear meat, venison, or roasted wild turkey, complemented by roasted ears of corn, potatoes, and the ever-present cornbread. All was served in a rudimentary style and eaten by people with vigorous appetites. By evening, the barn was finished and yet hardly anyone was too tired to enjoy a barn dance. Nearly every community had a fiddler who would bring his instrument as well as his tools, and would play foot tapping music for the occasion. The settlers would dance a round dance or other dance, depending on the talent of the musician. Often this celebration was held in the newly constructed barn.

Rail or stone fences separated the settlers' small clearings from the wild, and kept their crops and livestock safe from deer, wolves, and bears. Occasionally, there would be a mountain lion. According to geologists, Ohio shows signs of having been completely submerged in water at one time. Supposedly, north of the Great Trail was the end of the Glacial Drift, and south was water that was part of the Gulf of Mexico. When this water receded, the soil deposited was very rocky. Soil closer to the streams and rivers had a lot of clay. The rocks were abundant and could be formed into almost any shape. Since many of the stones had to be removed to plow the fields, settlers made fences with them and a few used them to build houses.

An example of a stone home still stands in its original location at the corner of the main street crossroads in Augusta (where State Route 9 and County Road 10 intersect). The sandstone was quarried from a nearby farm and built by John Manful. The masonry was done by Ellis Dunmore. Each stone was cut and dressed before construction began, then each was fitted perfectly in place as the house was built. It was the first stone house in the county. On the day of its completion, this stone house was considered one of the finest homes in the county.

The lifestyle of the settlers was plain, since most necessities and certain articles of food were difficult to obtain. Even though wild game was plentiful and cheap, pork was a more desirable diet, but the salt to cure the meat was difficult to obtain. Salt was essential for curing all meat, seasoning food, and for their livestock. But it had to be brought over the mountains from Pennsylvania on pack saddles. Salt was so scarce, it often cost $5 or more a barrel from the east. Daniel Clark of Fox Township retold a story of his father trading a three-year-old steer for a barrel of it. In 1809, the first salt well was put in near Salineville, Columbiana County. A short time later, more wells were drilled, and by the 1820s, salt could be purchased in Columbiana County. Later, Moore's salt works was established in Jefferson County. Shortly after the Civil War, in the late 1860s, salt was made at a well near Lisbon. The well had been drilled in hope of finding oil; instead, they struck natural gas and saltwater. They changed their plans and went to work making salt using the natural gas for fuel in burning down the saltwater. They made up to 30 barrels a day. Some of the farmers made an annual trip with their horses and wagons to the salt works near Lisbon, buying enough salt for a year.

Being so far away from the things they needed, early settlers were usually talented in a little bit of everything. They were carpenters, stone masons, brick layers, and cobblers. It was often necessary for the settlers to learn to make what they needed. They could make their own shoes from leather they had tanned. Brooms were made from broom-corn they had raised. Real maple syrup was made from the Sugar Maples in the area and candles were often made from tallow. These settlers became very self-sufficient. Their clothing was also homespun from flax they grew or wool sheared from their sheep.

When it was time to harvest these items, it was usually work-turned-fun. Corn husking, flax pulling, and log rolling were just a few of these events. Like the barn raising, neighbors worked together to get the job done and when it became too dark in the day to work, they celebrated with a meal and music, again provided by the fiddler or perhaps several attendees who would just sing. Settlers being so far apart, barn-raisings and harvesttime gave lonely neighbors a chance to visit, as well as help each other with their work.

Jesse Palmer is generally given credit as the first settler, although no one knows for sure. One of the first men to purchase land in the Carroll County area, Palmer came ahead of the immigration tide, in 1800, and settled what has since been called "Palmer's Fork." At the time, it was still part of Jefferson County, but is now Washington Township, Carroll County. While Palmer was building his log cabin, just south of him John Jackman was building a cabin along what was later called Elkhorn Creek in Lee Township. Elkhorn Creek got its name from a Mr. Reynolds, who later had a mill and tavern on the roadside near the creek. For his sign, he had used the antlers of an elk that measured over 12 feet in length. He called it the Elkhorn Tavern.

Later on this same creek, halfway between what is now Harlem Springs and Kilgore, another mill was constructed. It was built in 1837 by Jacob Winnings, and in 1840, No. 8 School was constructed nearby. The basement of the mill was a very cozy place with a fireplace designed for comfort of the patrons and guests. The room was sometimes used for social gatherings. The mill was used until 1898. The first miller was Michael Boop, who was succeeded by his son Jake. Josiah McConnell took over operation from the Boops and then George E. McConnell took over from him.

This site in Washington Township is the possible location of Jesse Palmer's farm. (Velma Griffin Collection.)

This image shows William Sherrod's home as it looks now. It was one of the first homes built in what would become Monroe Township. (Velma Griffin Collection.)

On a small plat of land across the creek from McConnell's house lived a Native American woman by the name of Polly Pipes. When she died, another neighbor, George Shepherd, attended her burial. The natives placed a tobacco pipe, a small piece of silver, and a few other small items in the grave with her. After a few years, the value of these items was exaggerated and the grave was robbed. McConnell then enclosed the grave in a pen of small logs notched together cabin-style.

Not long after Jesse Palmer and John Jackman, other settlers moved in and began establishing villages. John Jackman was soon joined by Jacob Gotschall, who moved from Berks County, Virginia to the Loudon Township area. Around 1802, Gotschall was joined by Maurice Albaugh, who settled 2 miles from what is now Kilgore. Albaugh's brother Peter, Daniel Shawver, Solomon Stine, Thomas Lucas, and Adam Simmons were soon building their cabins near Maurice's, but it would be another 32 years before the area would be platted by John Able. It was the first village platted (mapped or charted with actual proposed lots to be sold) after the formation of Carroll County. Originally, the area was part of Harrison County and the name Kilgore was chosen in honor of Daniel Kilgore of Cadiz, who was a member of Congress from that district. According to the plat book, John Able surveyed the land on December 17 and 18, 1834.

In the southern portion of what would become Carroll County, the first family was that of William Sherrod. A government scout for the Frontier line between the new nation and the unbound west, William Sherrod served as a kind of police patrol from Lake Erie to the Kentucky border. His main post was located in Virginia, across the river from Steubenville, and he was there to protect settlers from hostile natives. He served in this post for 16 years. Then, in 1804, when his duties ended, the government paid Sherrod $1,500 for his services. Leaving his married daughter in Wheeling, Sherrod and the rest of the family used the money to buy a farm 1 mile north of the present town of Sherrodsville. In time, he purchased eight more farms, one for each child. All except the one in Wheeling and a son David, who became a doctor and had his own farm.

At this same time, closer to the Leesburgh area, Abe Richardson staked his farm. Later, Thomas Price and his wife Sarah Rippeth came on horseback to the Kanotton (Conotton) Creek area, chose land near Abe Richardson, recorded their tract of land in Steubenville, and went to Kentucky for the rest of their family. One year later, on August 1, 1812, Price and Peter Saunders laid out the town of Leesburgh. They chose to name the town for Leesburgh, Virginia. It was officially platted on April 17, 1815. Together, the two men sold lots at auction.

Again, the village would not be platted right away; it would take another 14 years and it was not originally called Sherrodsville. In 1812, Conrad Pearch Sr. from Germany built the Pearch Flouring Mill along Kanotton (Conotton) Creek. The Pearch family owned most of the land near William Sherrod. Another German, George Peterson, built a home between Pearch's Mill and the William Sherrod farm. Situated on what is now the Monroe and Orange Township lines, Peterson laid out the village of Queensboro. It was platted March 24, 1817 and was mostly frame buildings instead of log. Queensboro was the seat of government for One-Leg Township and had two general stores, a hotel, and a blacksmith shop. The village was known for its wild, drunken brawls.

The actual platting of Sherrodsville began in 1882, about the time the Conotton Valley Railroad was built through the area. By 1884, a total of six plattings had been made and most came from the Pearch farm. The village was incorporated in 1888. When Carroll County was established and Monroe Township taken from Auburn Township in Tuscarawas County, the seat of Queensboro became a part of Sherrodsville. The survey of Sherrodsville was made by John and Allen Pearch. It was named for Charles Sherrod, the son of William Sherrod, who owned the rest of the land that created the village. He had a machine shop where he manufactured a small type of threshing machine. Charles's brother David introduced the pine tree to the area. Luther Pearch, John Pearch's son, started the first store in the village.

Sherrodsville was troubled by several fires. The first destructive fire was in 1890; it destroyed most of the businesses in the village. Everything was quickly rebuilt and business was back to normal. On August 11, 1911, 18 further buildings burned with a loss of $45,000; there was little insurance, as there was not enough fire protection for the area. Citizens from Carrollton, Leesville, and Bowerston arrived to try and help when news of the fire reached them, but very little was saved and most of the businesses were never rebuilt.

The fire started in the second story of Baxter Hardware and soon spread to Seeling Tailor Shop and Holcroft Restaurant. From there, it spread to German-Morrison Meat Market, and flames shot across the street and ignited the opera house. The only fire engine in the village failed. Accounts claim it barely had enough power to put out a fire in a stove. The entire business section on the south side of Mill Street, except for the Pearch building on the corner, was destroyed. In an attempt to save other buildings, the citizens tried to dynamite the Sherrodsville Supply Building, but failed, and Luther and Matilda Pearch's house was lost. Fortunately, many stock and household goods were removed from the buildings and saved. Those who did rebuild in the area constructed their buildings with brick.

Dedicated on January 1, 1906, Sherrodsville's City View Hospital stood on a high hill overlooking the village. It was built and operated by Dr. J. Dells Aldridge and included surgery and a nurse's training school. When Dr. Aldridge died, the hospital was torn down and moved to New Philadelphia.

A few miles southeast along the Kanotton (Conotton) Creek, also in One-Leg Township, Tuscarawas County, others began settling soon after Ohio was admitted into the Union in 1803. Benjamin Knight, Samuel Dunlap, and a few others built their log cabins on this creek between what is now Leesville and New Harrisburg. The creek and township were named for the previously mentioned one-legged native who lived in the area, Kanotton. Later, One-Leg Township was renamed Auburn.

In 1805, Captain James Downing returned to the area. He and son-in-law Isaac Van Meter came from Brooke County, Virginia and settled on government land near the site of Downing's encounter with the hostile Native Americans. The natives were much friendlier now and helped Downing build his first cabin. It is believed the change of heart in these natives was due to the Moravian missionaries of Schoenbrunn.

Captain Downing and Van Meter were joined by Richard Elson in 1834 and Isaac Miller, who named the village Downingville on March 22, 1836 in honor of Captain Downing. This was on the Carroll County side. While living in Virginia, Elson had traveled around the South, admiring the magnolias, and named his mill and flour after them. The portion of the settlement in Stark County was also called Magnolia. At some point, Downingville and Magnolia became one.

In 1806, Alexander Lee purchased a farm some miles from Jackman just north of what is now Harlem Springs. He was joined in December 1814 by William Van Horn and David Milligan. The same year, they laid out Millensburgh, as was transcribed in the *Carroll Book of Plats, Volume 1 from Harrison County Record Book A*. Joseph Wolff built a tavern here and called it Three Mile Tavern where travelers and their horses could be refreshed before continuing their 6-mile journey between Harlem Springs and Carrollton. David Lee operated a cheese factory not far from Wolff's and would haul his cheese in big, oxen-drawn wagonloads to Steubenville. The factory closed forever when the Civil War began. The only trace of the village is the Green Hill Cemetery, which sits back in the woods. Alexander's son Thomas inherited the area upon Alexander's death in 1819.

This image shows Sherrodsville's Mill Street before it was destroyed by the 1911 fire. (Velma Griffin Collection.)

The first settler in the Dellroy area, as far as is known, was James Davis. Settling in Warren Township, Tuscarawas County (now Monroe and Orange Townships, Carroll County) Davis, known as "Uncle Jimmy," built a sawmill on the Indian Fork of Kanotton Creek. He also built a small gristmill for grinding grain, which was entered by patent deed in 1806. It would take another 46 years for the area to be platted as Cannonsburgh, laid out in 1849 by Phillip Crabbs. When the post office was established, it was then called Leavitt/Cannonsburgh.

When the railroad came to the area in 1876, there was already a stop with the name Cannonsburgh, so it was decided this village should change its name. Legend has it that a traveling salesman spent the night at a local hotel and called the area "a royal dale." The people of the village decided this was a great name, but could not decide whether to call it Royal Dell or Dell Royal. President Cleveland's new bride called it Dellroy and this name was adopted.

The coal mines nearby brought the settlers to this village. Samuel Allen owned what was one of the largest mines in the area and built a large home just east of Dellroy. Today, this home is operated as a bed and breakfast called the Pleasant Journey Inn. In 1883, Dellroy had a hotel run by F.M. Ball, a dry goods store, carriage maker, grocery store, shoe shop, meat market, hardware store, and two blacksmiths. Today, there are many thriving businesses and churches in existence.

Monroe, a neighboring village, was never officially platted, just settled and given its name by Thomas James in 1850. Just 3 miles from Dellroy, it was also part of the coal mine era. In 1884, there were 2,214,000 bushels of coal mined out of Monroe Township. Without a major source of transportation through the area, Monroe never amounted to much. When the railroad forced Leavitt/Cannonsburgh to change its name, Monroe adopted the name of Leavittsville.

The first land deed in the Brown Township area was to Isaac Craig for 123 acres. On September 21, 1808, Isaac Craig and Amos Janney laid out the first recorded village, calling it Pekin. Soon after the village was laid out, they erected a small frame gristmill, which was propelled by a "tub" waterwheel. Many farmers used this mill, as it saved them a trip to the mill in Canton on horseback. Before it was erected, settlers used small hand grinders or pounded the corn into hominy. Soon afterward, though, a flood came and destroyed the dam that supplied water to the mill. The site was then sold to David and Jacob Crumbacker, who built a flour mill that served the community for several years.

Also settling on the banks of the Sandy Creek in 1808 were William Thompson and James Hewitt. The same year, James Knapp and Abraham Tidball made the first settlement where Oneida now stands. Oneida had a dominant role in the development of Brown Township because the town was an available source of waterpower. Another early settler of this area was builder Henry V. Bever. Oneida was not named until sometime after 1834, when brothers Patrick and George Hull settled near Sandy Creek and hired Bever to build a three-story gristmill. It is believed to be the only mill in the vicinity to grind buckwheat, operating until 1912. Shortly after the building was complete, George Hull returned to Oneida

An early postcard shows Main Street Dellroy facing east. The former Heatherland Restaurant was in the building on the left. (Courtesy Dan Rees.)

The Oneida Mill was built by Bever and Son. It changed owners many times before being destroyed by fire in 1875. (Velma Griffin Collection.)

County, New York where he married a Miss Shephard. Her father Jesse Shephard and his father Peter Hull came for a visit and named the Hull brother's mill Oneida Mills in honor of their home. Patrick Hull's home can still be visited and is part of the National Historical Society.

Credit for this community's growth belongs to Henry Bever and his son John. John was one proprietor of the Ohio Paper Mill. They also built a sawmill, woolen mill, and two-story gristmill and warehouse, which serviced shipping on the Sandy and Beaver Canal. By 1853, the Oneida gristmill was owned by James G. Fishel. Unfortunately, about 1875, the top floor was destroyed by fire. The entire structure was torn down in 1911. Oneida's second claim to fame was in 1882 when W.H. Morgan found a large tooth near the canal. It was believed to have belonged to a mastodon. Forty years later, two more teeth were found closer to Waynesburg along the Sandy Creek bottoms. Daniel Wagoner found two teeth that together weighed 15 pounds.

One year later, in 1809, John Reed and his family came from Pennsylvania to begin a settlement called Lodi, which is now the eastern portion of Malvern. This settlement was on the left bank of Sandy Creek. In the *Historical Atlas of Carroll County, OH*, William Hardesty tells the following about John Reed and his family:

> On their westward journey, they (the Reeds) stayed overnight near where McKaig's mill now stands on the west fork of Beaver Creek

> and from there they traveled 18 miles without passing a single human habitation, arriving at the house of Isaac Craig in Pekin. Travelers in those days of hospitality were gladly entertained by the pioneers who had preceded them and usually without charge.

(Most likely, McKaig's mill was in Columbiana County.)

Seven months after Craig and Janney laid out Pekin, Robert George moved from Washington County, Pennsylvania to what is now Scroggsfield. When he arrived, it is said, the only sounds were the birds and the wind through the trees. On April 4, 1809, he built a cabin for his family and stocked it with supplies. He then returned to Pennsylvania for his wife and infant daughter. When the family returned, the cabin had burned to the ground. George built another cabin where they lived until a brick house was built, thereafter they used the cabin for storage.

In 1815, George invited Reverend Elijah Newton Scroggs to come and preach in the vicinity. Worship generally took place under the shade of a tree. Reverend Scroggs noticed after several meetings that some listeners began to come by, complete with their guns and dogs. When they kept returning just to listen, Reverend Scroggs was encouraged by his labors, and remarking at the prospect of an early settlement, he considered the area a good "field" for the work he had undertaken. The term "field" in that context was new to the people and the locality soon became known as "Scroggs' Field," now one word, Scroggsfield. The reverend organized a religious society in 1818. At one time, Scroggsfield had a general store, school, blacksmith shop, post office, and gristmill on Strawcamp Run. By the mid-1890s, it also had a creamery. Scroggsfield was never officially platted, but is still recognized on the county map. Although it sits empty, the George home is still standing.

One of the men granted land, 1,000 acres, instead of pay for his service in the Revolutionary War was General James Ball. General Ball was a first cousin to George Washington, whose mother was Mary Ball. The Balls were Quakers and moved to the Leesburgh area sometime before 1809. That same year, a cemetery was started; in fact, it is the oldest recorded cemetery in the county. Along with building a log home, the Ball family also built a log church. When the Quakers moved west, the church became a temporary residence for other families traveling west. The church and cemetery were directly across the road from the Ball home.

Sometime in 1810, Peter Bohart, a Pennsylvania German, bought a farm from the federal government at Steubenville and built the first house in what is now Carrollton. He paid just $1.25 an acre. He was soon followed by George W. Butler, Samuel Bushong, Jacob Barkdal, James Sinclair, Alexander Leslie, Isaac Atkinson, Isaac Dwyer, Richard Elson, John Caskey, and William C. Croxton. On the opposite end of town from Bohart, Dwyer built a large log building, the Rising Sun Tavern, on Columbiana and Stark Counties' line. The line passed north and south through the house. When the Columbiana County Commissioners refused to give him a liquor license, Dwyer moved his bar into the room on the Stark County side.

About six years after building his home (now the site of Kiddieland Park on Park Avenue), Peter Bohart built a tavern at the crossroads leading from Steubenville to Canton and from Lisbon to New Philadelphia (site of the Bureau of Support Building today). It was another two years before he laid out the town of Centreville, Columbiana County on October 4, 1815. The name was derived from the area being equidistant between Lisbon, New Philadelphia, Canton, and Steubenville. The early settlers who settled near Peter Bohart had no idea that the area would someday be the seat of a new county.

Around the same time Bohart was in Centreville, Augusta was being laid out by Jacob Brown. It is believed he arrived in 1809, as that is the year he entered 320 acres in the Steubenville Land Office. He called this plat Brownsville and it was in Columbiana County. He built a log cabin, and in 1811, laid out a portion of the village. Later that year, he sold the first lot to a Mr. Rigglesworth. In 1812, he sold the remainder of his half-section to George P.S. Manful and a new frame house was erected in 1813. Other houses—log and frame—followed, and in 1815, the village had grown so well that the Pottotof Hotel was built. In 1817, A. Hayes started a general store. On June 17, 1859, an addition was made to the southern part of the village.

This side view of the brick Robert George home in Scroggsfield shows the basement where slaves were hidden. (Velma Griffin Collection)

This image shows an early photo of Market Street in Minerva, a settlement that was named after Minerva Ann, the oldest daughter of Pim Taylor and niece of John Whitacre. (Courtesy Dan Rees.)

While these folks were busy establishing their homes, villages, and mills, the War of 1812 was taking place to the North. Even though the United States had gained its independence from the British, they continued to be a problem. On the seas, the British attacked American merchant ships and forced the captured seamen to serve on the British naval ships. To Ohioans, the problem was that the British were manning forts throughout the country, aiding the natives by giving them supplies and encouraging them to attack the settlers.

The United States Congress officially declared war on England on June 17, 1812 and Ohio found itself right in the middle. Governor Retum Jonathan Meigs Jr. prepared by organizing a state militia. Fighting did not enter the land that would be Carroll County; however, the effects were felt as men from the Brown Township area were drafted into service. Men like John Thompson, William Reed, Henry Shultz, David Zimmerman, George Schultz, Caleb Knapp, and James Carrothers went into battle. Thomas and Joseph B. Tidbalt went also, but were underage and served as substitutes for others. After six months of service, these men reenlisted, serving a total of 18 months. On the journey home, John Thompson was wounded and died at Rock River. George Schultz came home ill and died within a few days.

Other men, who had already established themselves here, answered the call for troops as volunteers. Men from the Downing, Brown, Fulk, and Knott families in Rose Township, and James Reed, Robert Thompson, Samuel Knapp, John Creighton, Daniel Frederick, and George Fishel from Brown Township, all headed for Detroit. General William Hull was governor of the Michigan Territory, one of the areas the British were trying to control. It was Hull's job to hold Fort Detroit. He was getting old and his health was poor, so despite the willingness of his men to fight, Hull surrendered. The men from Rose and Brown Townships got as far as Sandusky when they were sent home. Having to walk, George Fishel died and was buried in the wilderness of the Sandusky area. The war ended in 1815 with the signing of the Treaty of Ghent, which set new boundaries, cleared up long-held disagreements between the two nations, and declared the Great Lakes to be neutral for the United States and Canada.

The War of 1812 only slowed the settling of the Ohio lands temporarily. During the spring of 1814, David Eakin moved to Brown Township and settled on land southeast of Oneida. There was a spring there and after being encouraged by several of his neighbors, Eakin began a distillery, which became a profitable investment, and a still-house was erected the next year. Whiskey was active in the market at that time for $1.50 per gallon. Corn and rye were only selling for $1 per bushel, so it may be inferred that whiskey manufacturing was much more profitable, especially since during this early period, liquor was kept as an article of entertainment by almost every family. When friends or neighbors met, it was always offered. If it was not offered, it was considered an insult. Eakin's distillery and still-house were the first in the county.

Stills were common in the early days of the county, since there was no revenue tax on liquors until the Civil War. Whiskey brought good, ready money to the farmer from the surplus grain crops. The men and boys who had taken a week's ride in a fox hunt usually wound up at one of these still-houses and replenished their jugs with corn and rye whiskey. Some would be made into tansy bitters and served at meals as a beverage. After 1870, there were no still-houses in Carroll County.

In 1815, Brown Township was made an independent township. It was originally part of Stark County and was named for John (or Jehu) Brown, who built the first mill. Brown was a Revolutionary War soldier who had served in Captain Daniel Morgan's company from Virginia in the expedition to Quebec under Colonel Benedict Arnold. In September 1813, he bought three lots in Pekin from Isaac Craig for the sum of $24. It was on this property that he had constructed his mill.

Another mill was built further upstream by John Whitacre, who worked as a surveyor. While surveying, he discovered a waterfall in Little Sandy Creek. He then purchased 123 acres, including the falls, from Isaac Craig. Whitacre then built the mill at the location of the falls. By 1828, a small cluster of log cabins sprung up around this mill. One of the early settlers was Pim Taylor, a teamster who operated a wagon train between Philadelphia and Mansfield, Ohio. Taylor married John Whitacre's sister Kisiah and they had 11 children. The oldest was a daughter whom they named Minerva Ann. Being the first child born in the settlement, Whitacre named it for his niece. (The former home of Minerva Ann and her ten brothers and sisters has been restored and is now a historic landmark in Minerva on East Plain

Street.) That same year, John Whitacre formed a partnership with John Pool and they built a new, two-story mill that stood until 1976. The lots sold by Whitacre were recorded in Stark County as Minerva and are located at the intersection of Stark, Carroll, and Columbiana Counties. The Sandy and Beaver Canal brought growth to this village in the 1840s. Later, the railroad had five stations, which led to Minerva being a manufacturing, agricultural, and trade center. Minerva was also home to Charles E. Wilson, who became president of General Motors and later secretary of defense in President Eisenhower's cabinet. President William McKinley visited often as he had a farm nearby known as the McKinley Tariff farm. Today, it remains a beautiful farm in Brown Township.

The first settlers to the newly independent Brown Township were Richard Vaughn and Moses Porter. Vaughn settled near Oneida, and Porter on the tract of land where the village of Malvern now stands. Being an independent township, the first election of officers was held in 1816. This resulted in the polling of the vote of every legal voter in the precinct, 29 in all. In the race for justice of the peace, 14 people cast votes for James Reed and 14 for Thomas Latta, while 1 was left blank. Since the vote was a tie, the judges of election proceeded to determine the matter by lot. James Reed was declared the winner and he held the position for 21 successive years.

Court cases of a severe matter were few and far between. All sorts of cases, except maybe grand larceny and murder, were the proper subjects of compromise between the contending parties. Assault and battery cases were usually ended by a handshake and both parties drinking from the "little brown jug."

Since the population was so sparse, the entire community was quick to know about it if an offense was made. Anyone who owed a debt, either in furs, whiskey, or powder, was reminded of it by everyone. If someone became ill, the whole community would do whatever it took to care for them. These settlers were very dependent on each other. Honesty was important in such dependency. At times, there were those who would take advantage of the other settlers and create problems. A man by the name of Wentchell was one of these people. Living in a cave south of Carrollton, he would steal horses and hide them in this cave. Several early settlers were robbed by him and men like him. Before the Civil War, horse stealing was very common. The stolen horses were again taken to the caves south of Carrollton. Two of the men responsible were caught and taken to New Hagerstown where they were hung.

Once government became more organized, settlers were eager to get involved. In 1816, the state representative from Tuscarawas County was Samuel Dunlap. This same year, on March 20, Dunlap platted the village of New Hagerstown in One-Leg Township, Tuscarawas County.

A nearby neighbor to Dunlap was John Fawcett. Settling on a government tract of land in 1816, John and his son Charles cleared the land to begin farming. The area was called "Little Ireland" since many of the early settlers were Irish. To obtain groceries and other necessities, John and two of his sons had to travel to Steubenville (30 miles) where they exchanged a load of wheat that had been

Called Navengall Hollow, these are the remains of the horse thief cave in Perry Township. (Velma Griffin Collection.)

thrashed with a flail (a hand instrument made of wood and used to thrash the wheat). Their nearest neighbor, George Tope, had built a gristmill and saved them the trip to Steubenville. The McGuire Fork is a branch of the Conotton Creek and flows through Union Township. This area is now called Petersburg.

Petersburg was not established until 1867. Tope built his gristmill in the valley, and a few years later, he built a long log house where he kept a little store he called Algonquin. This began the small village in Union Township. It was officially platted by George Tope's son Joseph and Cornelius Brackin on September 23, 1867. It was never recorded, though. Many of the residents referred to it as "Mudsock" until the roads were improved. The name Cornelius was often Americanized to Peter, so Dolly McCort thus named the area Petersburg in honor of Cornelius Brackin.

At one time, it was quite the manufacturing center with a sleigh, buggy, and wagon factory. There were two general stores, two blacksmiths, a gunsmith, cider press, and cooper shop. A hotel was operated by John R. King. The log mill was later replaced with a two-story frame structure that is now owned and operated by the Carroll County Historical Society. Every fall on the second weekend in October, the Algonquin Fall Festival is held to commemorate the mill and life of the early settlers. There are many buildings to visit and vendors supplying interested parties with crafts and foods of the pioneer style.

Sometime in the 1820s, the village of Oak Dale was platted, but the plat was never recorded. The name was changed to Atwood when the post office, kept by James Truman, was established. James Baxter had a store and undertaking establishment where the marker now stands along State Route 542. The town square was located at the intersection of State Route 542 and Monroe Township road 143. Just west of the marker was a United Presbyterian church, which is now the site of the current Yacht Club. The village had a band room and a band, a repair shop, cooper and furniture shop, and a town hall. There was a schoolhouse that doubled as a community center for many years. The building is now a summer home along the Atwood Lake. The village was discontinued in 1935 when the Muskingum Watershed Conservancy District built Atwood Lake in an attempt to prevent flooding. A marker commemorating this village was dedicated on November 16, 1986 by the Carroll County Historical Society.

Another village, of which this may be the only lasting record, was Winchester, made by John Swearingen in Harrison Township. Again, the plat was never recorded. Apparently, Winchester was never considered worthy of even building upon, according to different accounts.

By the 1820s, most of the land had been claimed and was still mostly wooded despite the clearing for so many farms. Settlers thought the forests would last for centuries. Most of the fields cleared were just for personal use until the completion of the canal in 1825, which brought the market much closer for grain crops, and extensive clearing took place. By 1900, 75 percent of the forests had been cleared. Then, all focus seemed to turn to transportation.

No longer standing, the Atwood Grocery is now remembered by a historical marker along State Route 542. (Velma Griffin Collection.)

3. The Canal Era and a New County

Once most of the villages had been established, the next need of the settlers was a sufficient way to obtain supplies. Most of the time, they were brought in on wagons from Pittsburgh, but with roads being little more than well-worn paths created by many wagon wheels and horse hooves, this was difficult. Each village had to become somewhat self-sufficient to accommodate the needs of its citizens. There was usually a mill, hardware and general store, tanner, saddlery, and harness maker in each village, as well as a blacksmith, wagon maker, carpenter, and hotel. But the items needed to keep these places in business could take days to obtain. A few things, especially new items, could be sampled in sample rooms. Salesmen would rent a small room and set it up to look like a store. Merchants from the smaller villages would then come to these sample rooms and order their needed items. This still did not answer the needs of the settlers themselves. As more people continued into the "west," a better means of travel was needed.

In 1811, the federal government built the Cumberland or National Road, which was 80 feet wide and cost as much as $13,000 a mile to build. The surface was made of crushed rock and was more like the "dirt" roads we know today. As it went from Cumberland, Maryland to Vandalia, Illinois, it helped get settlers to the western portion of Ohio. The merchants in Pennsylvania and Maryland did quite well, but it was still too far south to really help Carroll County's settlers.

This did not stop people from settling here though. Stagecoaches still found their way and were often the reason for a new village to begin. In 1820, Akey Worley built a tavern at the stagecoach crossroads to Bolivar, Canton, and Steubenville. The road followed the first white man's trail established by Belzaleel Wells, who founded the cities of Canton and Steubenville. The Worley tavern was halfway between Yellow Creek Hills and Bolivar. Even though most villages had mills, they often were not capable of keeping up with larger demands. Farmers would then take their wheat to large areas that could grind and provide a market for it. Farmers who were taking their wheat to Bolivar would often stop at the Worley Tavern.

Besides the Worley Tavern, there was also the Griffith Hotel and two saloons. One of the saloons was operated by Sealy Madden, who was known for doing her

The Park Hotel with sample rooms used to stand next to the courthouse. This area is now a parking lot. (Courtesy George Rankin)

own "bouncing" if a patron became unruly. Soon after these establishments, there was a drugstore, a wagon shop, four blacksmiths, a cigar-making establishment, a general store, and an iron ore pit with several mines nearby. During the stagecoach days, this new village had 1,500 residents. A Catholic mass was begun in the home of John Waggoner in 1828, and on August 24, 1831, he and Samuel Oswalt platted the village as Moregg. It is now called Morges.

The stagecoach line ran to Leesburgh along what is now Azalea Road and jogged around to New Hagerstown and Bowerston before going on to Scio and Steubenville. This line often carried supplies from Baltimore, Maryland to the area until Steubenville became a buying and selling market. Long before the railroad, anything coming in or out of a village came by stagecoach. For speedy mail delivery, an express form of overland coach was designed, called the Pony Express. The ponies were changed often and the coach came into the business districts of each village to deliver the mail. The last run of the Pony Express was during the Civil War.

Unfortunately, villages like Morges began to dwindle when the Ohio Commissioners decided to build canals on January 8, 1825. "An act to provide for the internal improvement of the State of Ohio by Navigable Canals" was started. On February 4, 1825, construction of Ohio's canals began. The Canal Act opened a whole new way to travel.

The largest canal was the Ohio and Erie, which ran from Lake Erie in Cleveland to the Ohio River at Portsmouth. It was about 110 miles long and connected to the Erie Canal on the other side of Lake Erie. This opened trade and commerce to central Ohio.

The same year, a canal to run through Columbiana County, connecting the Pennsylvania and Ohio Canal at Glasgow, Pennsylvania to the Ohio and Erie at Bolivar, was proposed. It was accepted and called the Sandy-Beaver Canal because it joined the Sandy Creek in the west with the Beaver Creek in the east. Both of these creeks served as the canal's primary source of water. Construction on the Sandy-Beaver was begun in 1835.

Once it was built, the Sandy-Beaver Canal entered Ohio at East Liverpool and entered the Carroll County area in Minerva. It then went southwest through Pekin and Lodi. When William Hardesty heard the canal would definitely pass through the area, he platted a town and called it Troy. For ten years prior to this plat, the only way to cross the Sandy Creek at this point was by ferry. Then, Isaac Miller built Miller's Bridge. Troy combined with Lodi to become Malvern. A toll station was located here to allow boats to wait for passage through the locks. It was a halfway point between Minerva and Waynesburg. Brown Township contained Miles 51 through 54 of the Sandy-Beaver Canal.

Mile 51 and Lock No. 12 were a half-mile west of Pekin. The canal entered the creek and was backed up by Dam 2. The canal crossed the creek above the dam and went on the left bank through a field where Lock 14 was, 100 yards east of the creek.

Mile 52 was the position of Dam 3, which was constructed of stone on the left bank of the creek and earth walls on the right bank. Here, timbers were placed

Taken during the Canal Days, this photograph shows a remnant of the Sandy-Beaver Canal, which still exists in Magnolia.

in the creek for support. The canal crossed the creek above the dam on the right side. The stone Lock 15 was at Minerva Junction, where the railroad crosses the canal. Lock 17 was just south of Oneida. The creek has since broken into the canal walls and the two are now one. On careful examination, you may still see the stone remains of the canal.

Mile 53 is where Dam 4 and Lock 19 were placed. The dam was made of timber with stone abutments. The lock was on the right bank.

Mile 54 was located at Troy, now Malvern, and was the position of Lock 20. Eberhart's *Atlas of Carroll County* (1874) shows that a woolen mill had been built right over the dam at this location and a gristmill to the south. From there, the canal passed through Magnolia and on to Bolivar where it joined the Tuscarawas River, which could then be traveled south to the Ohio. The Sandy-Beaver Canal Company was formed in 1828 with the headquarters in New Lisbon (Lisbon), Ohio where some of its most eager backers lived.

Built by private and mostly local funding, the canal was intended to provide a direct route from the Ohio River to the Ohio and Erie Canal on the Tuscarawas River at Bolivar. Locks were built using handhewn sandstone from local quarries, such as one located on Pine Hill near Minerva. Measuring approximately 1.5 feet square, up to 8 feet long, and weighing 3,000 pounds, the stones were transported anywhere from 3 to 5 miles by oxen or mules to their destinations.

When it was completed, the Sandy-Beaver was 73 miles long with 30 dams and 90 locks. It was divided into three divisions: eastern, middle, and western. The western division was in this portion of Ohio, and along with the eastern division, was very prosperous. The middle division had structural problems, and therefore the full potential of the canal was never realized. It is said that the only boat to make the entire trip was the contractors', who were compelled to push on to fulfill a contract. It is also said that this boat had to be pulled through mud to achieve its goal. Even though the stockholders did lose about $2 million, we know from

This marker shows the location of the Sandy-Beaver Canal as it passed through Minerva. The stones holding the markers were taken from Lock 15 in East Rochester, Ohio.

The Stage Coach Inn was a general store where residents brought butter and eggs to trade for sugar, spices, and coffee, and had a chance to find out what was happening in the rest of the world—before it became an inn. (Velma Griffin Collection.)

later accounts that the canal was indeed used. It served as a feeder for many mills along its banks, but was officially abandoned in 1850 mainly because railroad travel became more popular.

Construction of this canal opened trade for Carroll County settlers. Before the canals, pioneer farmers had very little market for any surplus wheat nearer than the Ohio River. With the canals, the farmer could haul surplus wheat to Massillon, Bolivar, or other canal ports—usually a two-day journey. Wheat then became a cash crop; if the price was good, the farmer could receive $1 a bushel. Wheat would often be stored at home until after a good sledding snowfall and then taken to Bolivar on sleds. Little bridges were constructed to cross the smaller streams.

Perhaps as important as the actual use of the Sandy-Beaver for transportation was the leasing of water rights for the many mills constructed along its course. The elevations between the locks provided excellent sites for millwrights to erect mills and a considerable diversity of milling activity used the waterpower.

In anticipation of the coming canal, the town of Wiertemburg was laid out on the left bank of the Sandy Creek across from Oneida by John G. Hudlemeyer on September 29, 1836. Yet, when the canal actually came through, it was on the right bank closer to Oneida. Wiertemburg then became the south side of Oneida when it began to build up in 1853. The area is now the group of houses along State Route 183 to the south of Oneida.

The stagecoaches carried passengers to the canal. It was still quite a distance and it was usually necessary for stop-overs along the way. New villages developed out of these stop-overs; for example, New Harrisburg. On April 21, 1827, Jacob Harsh platted this village. In 1828, the Stagecoach Inn opened on the corner of Sandy Street (so named as it led to the Big Sandy in Malvern) and the current State Route 171. The two-day journey to either the markets at Bolivar or Canton,

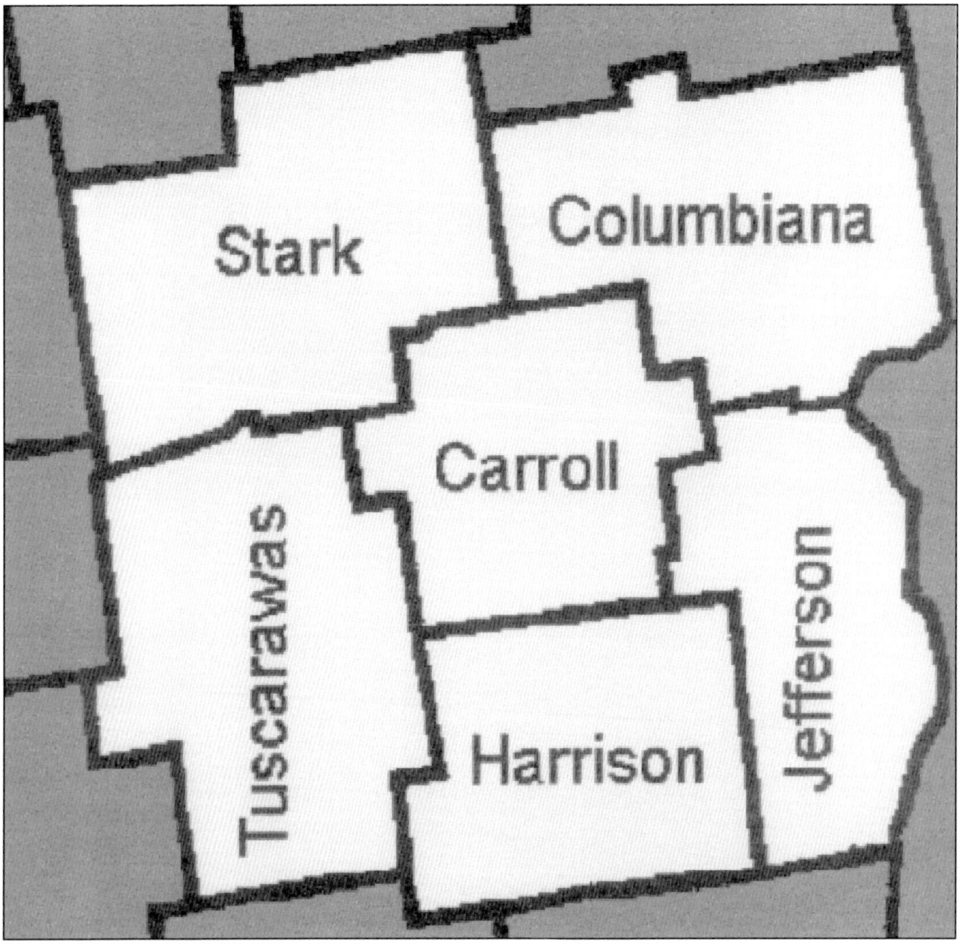

This map shows the addition of Carroll County; if compared to the 1814 map (page 18), one can see which portions were removed from the other counties.

especially since the mill at Pekin was only big enough to accommodate the needs of the immediate vicinity, made it necessary for farmers to travel just to have their own wheat ground. So, a stop-over in New Harrisburg was convenient for them as well.

There were other villages that seemed to develop for no real reason. One such village was Valdarno, laid out on September 22, 1827 by J.W. Candy, according to the *Book of Plats, Volume 2*. The only other information on this village also comes from the *Book of Plats* and says that it was situated on land owned by Jonathan M. Candy in Stark County. It was two rods north from a white oak, marked for a corner in the middle of the road leading from Wellsville on the Ohio River, to the Sandy-Beaver canal on the west bank of Clear Fork on Sandy Creek.

Just prior to the forming of Carroll County, the village of Harlem Springs in Lee Township was laid out by Isaac Wiggins. The original plat was filed on March

15, 1832 in Harrison County and it was simply called Harlem. Wiggins platted an addition to the village on August 31, 1840. There was no major transportation source to the area, but the natural springs attracted many people. It had evidently been named in honor of Haarlem, Holland as the mineral waters at Harlem Springs must have reminded some settler of the famous spring of chalybeate (water impregnated with iron) in old Haarlem.

There were four types of mineral water in this area: magnesia, sulfur, iodine, and spring. These springs led to the opening of a spa resort that was very popular before and after the Civil War. With the lack of medicines that we know today, these "healing" waters drew great crowds. People from all parts of the country would come to drink this water. Men such as Confederate General Robert E. Lee, the Honorable Edward M. Stanton (President Lincoln's secretary of war), and President William Henry Harrison visited these springs. The resort was first operated by Isaac Wiggins's son Abel. He sold the resort in 1850 to Sarah Bierdemann, who died shortly after buying. In November 1851, it was purchased from her estate by John Hilbert.

Hilbert let the world know that he had taken over by announcing it in many newspapers. One of the big things he bragged of was the hydropathic physician who had been employed. The resort also had a bowling alley and a prototype of a ferris wheel. In 1856, Hilbert sold the resort to Simpson S. Hart for $3,500. Hart operated it for a year before he sold to William McCoy. By the end of the Civil War, the water had lost a lot of its iron content and the town went from a resort to an educational center. To accommodate students, the resort became a dormitory. When the college closed, Harlem Springs became a quiet farming community. Unlike other villages platted at this time, Harlem Springs has remained fairly strong and is one of the few to still maintain its own post office. Although the springs are gone, water from the underground wells in this area still contain a high concentration of iron.

On September 4, 1832, the only village in East Township was platted. Known as Norristown, it was platted by Daniel Norris and only had a handful of residents. The early families were the Norrises, Bakers, and Battins, each moving to the area sometime after September 17, 1808. For awhile, it had its own school, but once that was consolidated into the public school system of Carrollton, Norristown became something of a ghost town.

A few days later on September 24, John Rice settled a couple miles south of Scroggsfield and called his settlement Woodsberry. Like Valdarno and Norristown, this area never materialized into anything more than a name in the history books. It was recorded in the *Book of Plats, Volume 1* and was transcribed from the *Jefferson County Record Book-N*. Had the citizens of the entire area not pushed to have a new county formed, these little areas may have been completely forgotten and the citizens of the existing villages would most likely be traveling to another county to pay taxes and do other court business.

The first action toward establishing a new county, of which there is any record, was on December 14, 1818. The state House of Representatives records show that Jefferson County Representative Stephen Ford presented a petition by the citizens for the establishment of a new county to be taken from Columbiana, Stark, Tuscarawas, and Jefferson Counties. The Senate was then informed of this request and the motion was denied. Nothing happened until Peter Bohart died in 1825 and Isaac Atkinson purchased his entire estate. Atkinson built a gristmill, oil mill, and carding machine, all at first propelled by yoke of oxen on a tramp wheel. Later, this was changed to steam and the gristmill became one of the first steam mills west of the Ohio River. Atkinson not only became a prominent businessman at this time, he also began lobbying for the new county. He tried for at least six years.

Each winter, Atkinson would travel by horseback to Columbus to try to convince officials that a new county needed to be formed. After spending a little over $7,000, and during his seventh winter in Columbus, Atkinson discovered that one of the influential members of the Senate, who had taken a stand against the bill, had a brother-in-law who kept a tavern in Columbus. Atkinson went to the brother-in-law and told him how long and hard he had been trying to get the bill passed and asked the man to try to change the senator's mind. It was promised to the senator that if the bill passed, Atkinson would host a banquet at the tavern for the members of the assembly, the state officials, and the prominent men of the state.

On Christmas Day, 1832, the stubborn senator changed his mind and the bill passed both houses. As promised, Atkinson held his banquet. When the news reached the citizens of the new county, the usually calm and collected people became wild with delight. A bonfire was kindled and the people marched through the streets. People of all ages were heard shouting. Henry Stidger fired his cannon, which was said to be heard a quarter-mile away. This cannon sat near the alley along Honey Run, a small creek that runs across Main Street behind the courthouse, Myer's Tin Shop, and the Bureau of Support. Honey Run was mostly filled in and now runs completely underground. Stidger's cannon sat along this creek until 1860 when President Buchanan's secretary of war ordered it to be sent to the South.

The act also named Centreville as the county seat. A few citizens wanted it to be in New Harrisburg, but when Isaac Atkinson donated the land to build the courthouse, it was agreed that the seat would be Centreville. The legislation formed Carroll County from the five neighboring counties just as Stephen Ford had originally proposed. From Stark County, the townships of Brown, Rose, and Harrison were given to Carroll. Columbiana County gave Augusta, Franklin, Washington, and Fox. The name of Franklin was changed to East. Portions of Warren and Auburn Townships in Tuscarawas County became Monroe and Orange, respectively. Harrison County parted with Rumley, Rock, and North, which later became parts of Perry, Union, Loudon, Lee, and Orange. The remaining portions of Lee and Loudon came from Jefferson County. There were two townships: Clinton and Springfield. At the March 1836 meeting, the county commissioners ordered a township named Centre to be erected from parts of Washington and Harrison Townships, which included Carrollton.

On January 9, 1833, another act was passed by the state congress. This act changed the name of Centreville to Carrollton in honor of Charles Carroll. The newspaper changed its name from the *Centreville Recorder* to the *Carrollton Gazette*. When General Henry A. Stidger told Carroll of the name choice, it's said that he smiled and said he greatly appreciated the compliment. He died six months later as the last surviving signer of the Declaration of Independence. The act changing the name also stipulated when and how a local government was to be formed.

On February 22, 1833, the law creating the new county of Carroll was put into effect and the first county officers were elected. The election resulted in the following: John Beatty, sheriff; Thomas McGavran, coroner; John Shober, William Davis, and James Ferrall, commissioners; David Workman, treasurer; George Beatty, auditor; Aquilla Jones, recorder; William Brown, assessor; and Van Brown, surveyor.

The first term of court and the first sessions of the Carroll County commissioners were held in Peter Bohart's tavern, then owned by David J. Levy. They met there a few times before renting the Lutheran Reformed Church on East Main Street. David Workman held the treasurer's office at a home where the Bargain Outlet store is now. (This was the J.C. Penney building for years.)

The Honorable John Pearce was the presiding judge with George Davis, George Reynolds, and Robert George as associate judges. Daniel McCook was clerk of the new county. Until 1836, the portions of Carroll County taken from the other five counties voted for representatives with their original counties. The state was then reapportioned and Carroll County was allowed a representative of its own. As an acknowledgment of his untiring services of more than six years in obtaining the county, Isaac Atkinson was elected its first representative to the Ohio legislature.

When it came time to build the courthouse, the businessmen at that time gave the greater part of the money from their own private funds. *Commissioners' Journal*

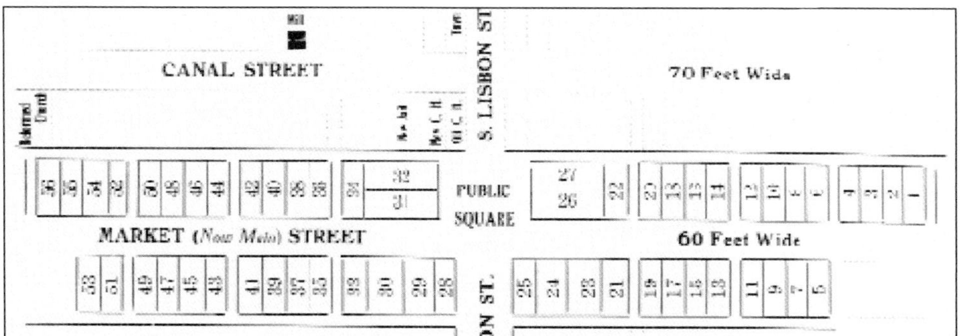

The original plat map of Centreville, now Carrollton, is shown here as it was laid out by Peter Bohart.

A shows that when the commissioners went to the state bank at Steubenville to borrow the money to complete the courthouse and pay the contractor, the bank refused to accept their promise to pay until George W. Butler endorsed their note.

John M. Lacy of Cadiz received the contract for building the courthouse and jail. The brickwork was laid in what is called Flemish Bond style and the jail was completed first. After Lacy completed the jail and his wife had done the plastering they refused to finish the job. The first journal of the county commissioners shows that a Mr. Forbes was sent to Cadiz to see Lacy. Then it was ordered that the contract be re-let to George Y. Thompson, who employed Peter Herold Sr. to do the carpentry work. William Johnston Esq. was authorized to draw the plans and specifications.

While the preliminaries were going on, Isaac Atkinson and Daniel McCook were making the bricks upon their land on West Canal Street (now Second Street SW behind the home of Carl and Ann Saltsman). The bricks were then hauled by oxen, upon a wooden track laid from the brickyard to the public square. From these same bricks, Daniel McCook built his own home. After the completion of the building and the cupola, in 1835, the town subscribers to the building fund

Taken by Port C. Baxter and originally published in the Centennial Book, *this photo shows the old and new courthouses.*

This was the county jail for many years. It was replaced with a new complex in 1975. (Courtesy George Rankin.)

were called upon for settlement. William Runion plastered the jury rooms and the offices were assigned. The commissioners' journal shows where installments of $50 and $25 were paid upon the courthouse bell, made at the Fulton Bell Foundry in Pittsburgh, sent by boat to Wellsville, and hauled here by Fleming Dempster. The journal also shows that Joshua D. Patton was employed to paint the court house and that David Albaugh was paid $4 for ringing the courthouse bell. In the way of supplies for the courthouse, "Spit boxes, ink, sand, wafers, candles, etc." were ordered. The journal shows that A.L. Littel was paid for making post-and-rail fences at the jail. The jail locks were provided for as well. The site of this courthouse is marked by its bell, which still stands on the public square.

The first convict sent to the penitentiary from Carroll County was Solomon Harding, who was indicted for incest, found guilty, and sentenced for a term of eight years. Robert McClure Esq. acted as prosecuting attorney, appearing for the state, and William Johnston Esq. represented the prisoner. The trial was held in the unfinished courthouse and the crowd of spectators was so large that the floor was rendered unsafe; it afterwards sank 3 or 4 feet with the large crowd that assembled to hear an address delivered by Thomas Corwin.

In 1885, the courthouse was razed and a new one was built of Berea Sandstone. A brick jail and sheriff's residence were also constructed for $150,000. The cornerstone was laid May 22, 1885. The current courthouse has undergone many changes internally over the years, but its only exterior change has been the color of the bell tower.

Now A.R. Elson Lumber, this mill was built by Richard Elson in 1834 along the Sandy-Beaver Canal. (Courtesy Dan Rees.)

A new addition was added in 1884, in the lower southwest corner. This was a large ladies waiting room with restrooms. The waiting room had long solid oak tables and chairs where women would knit, exchange recipes, and gossip while their husbands conducted business elsewhere in the building. Young girls would go there to do their homework and it also served as a preparation place before attending community parties. By the 1990s it was only a restroom and after September 11, 2001 it was closed completely and that corner of the courthouse is now the treasurer's office.

In November 1973, the courthouse was listed on the National Register of Historic Places. In April 1974, the jail was razed and a new justice center constructed. This justice center houses the jail, commissioners' offices, sheriff's office, and many other important county offices.

With the establishment of the new county, more villages were being laid out: the first after the formation was Kilgore, which was followed by Minerva and then the little town of Perrysville. Perrysville was platted by Mahlon Stewart on his 464-acre farm January 28, 1835. A first addition was made on October 20, 1846 and when a second addition was made, 11 lots were added. In 1900, a fire broke out in a fabric store that stood next to the present township building. Everything on this west side was destroyed. The fire was believed to have been started by the owners of the fabric store. The owners went to the store, and a short time later, were seen walking out of the building. After this, townspeople saw flames coming from the building. The fire was fought by a bucket brigade that was formed from the bottom of the hill where Perry Post is now. The townspeople rebuilt and the town thrived until the 1930s when the Great Depression forced the closing of most of the local businesses. Perrysville was also known as Lamartine when the post office was established.

In 1836, when Magnolia was platted, Elson's Mill was thriving. The mill still stands today and has remained in the Elson family since Richard built it in 1834. He operated it until 1881 when his son Augusties R. Elson took over. Augusties ran it for 30 years before turning operations over to his three sons, Richard, John, and Frank. In 1947, it was passed on to the next generation of Elsons, Mack and Lorene. Today, it is owned by Mack Elson's three children. Thanks to an active Canal Society, a Canal Days Festival is held every August commemorating the life and activities of the 1800s. A portion of the canal remains at Elson's Mill.

In the year 1836, Thomas McGavern platted Mechanicstown, also known as Mechanicsburg. Situated 9 miles northeast of Carrollton, by 1880, this village had a population of 200. Also at that time, there were three churches, two sawmills, a general store, physician, hardware store, cobbler, undertaker, millinery, postmaster, and agricultural implements store. Although there are not as many businesses there now, the village of Mechanicstown is still thriving.

The village of Bassora was laid out by William Croxton Jr. on March 27 and 28, 1837. It was recorded in the *Book of Plats 4* on April 7, 1837. The land deed says a basin was left between lots 33 and 27. This basin was "in case the canal be made along its western margin." The canal never came close and perhaps that was why the area never developed.

This aerial view of Mechanicstown is from a postcard owned by Dan Rees. The photo was taken from an old church bell tower on the east side of town looking west. The small building in the center was the blacksmith's shop.

In 1838, another plat was made 10 miles from Carrollton. On March 27, David Watt platted Wattsville. In 1880, it was reported that this little place had a general store, two sawmills, a shoe shop, a blacksmith, and a physician, as well as a population of 50. The population was the same in 1920. At some point, the stores closed and the physician left. The population has dwindled, but there is not an exact count at this time.

A few months later, on July 17, George K. McCaskey platted the village of Palermo 8 miles south of Carrollton. Its population in 1880 was only 15 people. Most of the services here were operated by S.T. Allen. He operated the general store, the blacksmith shop, and the only tavern in the village, as well as being postmaster. McCaskey was a farmer in the area. The Methodist church here was called the "New Side" Methodists in opposition to the southern supporters at "Confederate Crossroads" further south in the same township.

One of the remnants of the early travelers through Carroll County was a stone less than a mile from the first white man's grave. Carved deeply into the stone were the words, "I am now 200 mi from home. Your E-N [the N was reversed] H-B 1847." There was nothing more. One can only wonder from where this person had traveled, as 200 miles at that time would have been most likely from the east at that date; the stagecoach from Steubenville to Canton passed just a few hundred yards from the stone. Perhaps a weary traveler felt the need to make his mark while waiting for the stage to be repaired or while the horses rested. We will never know, but E-N H-B is definitely remembered.

It would be 11 years after Palermo before another plat was made. It was the plat of Cannonsburgh (Dellroy) followed by Monroe (Leavittsville). The last known plat was Pattersonville on November 15, 1907. It was platted by George S. Patterson. Only a few houses remain to remind us of this plat.

There are many citizens who have traveled to various parts of the world, but none had the effect that a traveler to Australia had on the Mechanicstown area in the 1960s. A couple of men were sitting at the local gas station chatting about the trip and a very gullible young man came along. They told the young man that the traveler had brought back a kangaroo as a souvenir, but it had gotten loose. Supposedly, this kangaroo was hiding near the railroad bridge over State Route 39. To this day, the railroad bridge is called Kangaroo Crossing.

4. All Aboard!

Even though canal travel helped farmers procure needed items, it often meant making a journey of many miles over the roughest roads or without roads at all. Farmers were often forced to camp amid unknown dangers only to discover they still were not able to get the needed items; either they were not available or the expense was too great. As late as 1835, there was no general market for produce nearer than Steubenville, although wheat could be sold at Zoar, Bolivar, or Massillon. So, when the railroads began, they brought tools and supplies of all kinds practically to the farmer's front door.

This made the canal era short-lived, especially since it was responsible for hauling in supplies to build the railroad. Once it was completed, rail travel was much more convenient and popular. In the 1830s, the Carrollton & Lodi Railroad Company got permission to build a railroad from Carrollton to the Sandy-Beaver Canal. It was never built due to a panic in 1837 and its stocks could not be sold. In 1846, the railroad changed its name to the Carroll County Railroad Company and tried to raise funds again. They still failed. Eventually, a line was completed using out-of-date stock.

The first depot in Carrollton was a frame building erected in 1853 that was destroyed by fire in 1876. It was replaced by another frame building in 1880, built by John G. Byder. This building was sold to Dewey Lewton in March 1913 for $85 and it was decided then to build the present brick structure. Both of the earlier depots were located closer to Main Street. The depot is now owned by Carroll Rail, Inc., which operates an excursion train from Carrollton to Minerva called the Elderberry Excursion Line.

The first line through the county was the Tuscarawas branch of the Cleveland & Pittsburgh Railroad, which passed through Brown Township by way of Minerva, Pekin, Oneida, and Malvern. The branch was constructed in 1853 and 1854, and the Carrollton & Oneida Railroad was put in operation a short time later, connecting with the Tuscarawas Branch at Oneida, 10 miles from Carrollton. The first train on the Carrollton Line was on May 24, 1852. It had one car and was pulled by horses. The road was very crude, made of wooden rails 6 inches thick, 8 inches wide, and in length ranging from 8 to 16 feet. Along the upper side of these was a line of strap-iron half an inch thick and 3 inches wide, fastened down

This is a depiction of the horse-drawn train that was first used by the Carrollton & Oneida line. (Photo from the Centennial Collection.)

with spikes driven about 5 feet apart. This early train was called the Elderberry Special. The story is, a man would pick the elderberries along the trip as the train was slow going. He said he got a tub full each trip.

The Cleveland and Wellsville Road at first operated the Carroll County Road on shares, running from Bayard to Oneida, then to Carrollton, and return. Later, when the Cleveland & Wellsville branch along the Sandy Valley was completed, that road discontinued its arrangement with the Carroll County Road and the local company bought an engine in New York in 1855. It was an old one that had been built in England and brought to the United States for a pattern. In 1859, this line saw no profit and was sold by the sheriff to John Ebersole, Henry A. Stidger, James Huston, James P. Cummings, Jacob Helfrich, and James Cameron. This sale, however, did not include the locomotive, which was the personal property of the president of the road. A small amount of rolling stock was purchased and horsepower was resorted to. The road was operated by horsepower until 1866 when the road was rebuilt and equipped with a locomotive built in Cleveland. The fare was 75¢ between Carrollton and Oneida, but business consisted largely of freight traffic.

In 1873, this branch was changed to the Ohio & Toledo Railroad Company, and was a narrow gauge road that ran from Oneida to Minerva and from Carrollton to Cannonsburgh (Dellroy). Proposals were made by the Ohio & Toledo Railroad Company to extend the track into the new coal fields, equip the road with "T" rails, and put on first-class rolling stock, with the ultimate purpose of extending the railroad tracks all the way to Toledo or to some other Lake Erie port. The

The Ohio & Toledo train is shown here crossing the bridge in Oneida. (Courtesy Carroll County Historical Society.)

new company was given the old roadbed of the Carrollton & Oneida Railroad and the local community in Carrollton was asked to subscribe $45,000 in stock to share the cost. Everything was secured and General Ephraim R. Eckley became president of the company.

After many tribulations and the failure to collect much of the stock subscription, General Eckley succeeded in getting a narrow-gauge track, which operated between Carrollton and Minerva, extended south to Dellroy. In 1877, E.G. Livermore, a New York banker, invested in the road and put N.A. Smith in charge. Smith put the road in first-class condition and extended the tracks to Sherrodsville.

General Eckley found himself ousted and broke, as far as the railroad was concerned. Many lawsuits against the railroad followed, and on November 27, 1878, under court order, the road was sold to the highest bidder. Purchased in the interest of the Smith party, the Cleveland Iron Company was that high bidder. The line was then extended to Canton under the name of the Youngstown and Conotton Valley, which was later changed to the Conotton Valley.

In 1881, this road acquired pieces of track leading from Canton to Zanesville, and set out building connecting links. The main line was extended to Cleveland in 1883, and at this time, the Conotton Valley handled 192,000 tons of coal, 41,000 tons of freight, and 456,686 passengers. Shortly after the line was extended in 1883, it met Coshocton. On May 15, 1885, the Conotton Valley Railway was sold at Special Master Commissioners Sale on the courthouse steps in Canton. It was purchased by Albert N. Parlin, on behalf of William J. Rotch, who became president of the company. Joseph B. Thomas, William O. Chapman, and Parlin comprised the Board of Reorganization trustees of the road. These men were from Boston, Massachusetts. On June 25, 1885, the name was changed to Cleveland and Canton.

There were 63 miles of railroad in Carroll County at this time. The line was narrow gauge until Sunday, November 18, 1888 when it was changed to standard gauge. Men from all parts came to help, and by changing every third tie, the entire line was changed in one day. The rail extension to Zanesville was completed in 1889 and the name again changed to the Cleveland, Canton & Southern. The name was once again changed July 26, 1899 to the Wheeling & Lake Erie Railroad (W&LE).

The Wheeling & Lake Erie provided passenger service from Sherrodsville, Dellroy, Carrollton, Hibbets, and Minerva. Picking up passengers in Minerva, the train would continue back through Oneida and on to Robertsville, East Canton, and Cleveland. There were three depots in Minerva. The first depot was originally a wood structure with slate siding, located on Market Street and owned by the Pennsylvania Railroad, which was best known for its passenger transportation. It was still standing until the early 1970s. This line was constructed through Magnolia in 1854. One was the New York City freight depot on Valley Street. It was torn down in 1958. The Baltimore & Ohio line was built through the Magnolia area in 1899. The current depot was erected about 1915 by the W&LE, also on Valley Street. North & West had a traveling agent using the depot

The current train depot at Carrollton which is now home to the Elderberry Excursion Line.

This image shows Main Street in Augusta during the late 1870s, before the railroad came through.

until 1980, at which time it closed. The depot sat unused and vandalized until 1991 when a new W&LE took over 550 miles of line in Ohio and Pennsylvania. Ohi-Rail, the village of Minerva, and Kohman Ford got together and purchased the depot from W&LE. Ohi-Rail removed the track leading to the depot and cut in a new switch reconnecting the old Pennsylvania Railroad with the old W&LE in Minerva. The village received a grant, fixed up the depot, and it now houses the chamber of commerce and the Salvation Army. A waiting room is also open for passengers of the Elderberry Excursion Line train.

The Elderberry Excursion Line began when a current owner thought about purchasing the Carrollton Depot for personal use. In 1993, the W&LE abandoned their line, which ran from Canton to Carrollton. Six local residents and two businesses joined together to keep the line open. It was leased from W&LE. The first run was made in 1997 and was named for the earlier Elderberry Special.

The railroad through Augusta was a boost to the local economy. The right of way was obtained by the Cleveland, Youngstown, and Pittsburgh Company for the new railroad in late 1882. In early 1883, it was built and operated for a period of time by this company. This railroad supplied a means of transportation that was far ahead of what they had at this early time. It also created employment for many of the local citizens. Quite a few made it a lifetime occupation. The taxes paid by the railroad also helped the county and township financially. In 1884, the appraised value of the new railroad was $4,000 per mile and the rolling stock $1,000 per mile, which would have generated $800 in tax for the county for one year.

When railroad service was discontinued, Wathey's Station was moved to the Algonquin Mill in Petersburg and restored.

On July 31, 1886, the railroad was sold to a committee of creditors for $100,000, and on January 28, 1887, a new board of directors was appointed and the name of the company changed to Lake Erie, Alliance & Southern. In 1902, the year the new depot was built, the road was operating under the name Lake Erie, Alliance & Wheeling. A short time later, it was changed to the Lake Shore, Michigan & Southern and finally to New York Central. The first stop from the Stillfork Valley on the railroad after leaving Minerva was at a place called Cat Fish Pond, where a station and a warehouse were located. The next stop was Pattersonville, which was called Augusta Station by the railroad company. The station was a small building, which was replaced in 1902 by a new and larger passenger and freight depot on the opposite side of the public road.

After Pattersonville, the train would go to Wathey's and then another mile or so to a small building erected near the railroad at Hewitts Crossing. It was erected by William F. Specht, who maintained a post office there and who had also established a general store on December 8, 1890. This area was thus named Specht. In 1893, a creamery and cheese factory called Gold Spring Creamery was built at Specht by a stock company of local citizens. The board of directors consisted of president Wesley Snively, secretary William F. Specht, treasurer J.C. Patterson, Jason Kennedy, and Eli Crawford. The creamery and cheese factory was in operation for an unknown period of time before William F. Specht bought them out. Specht and Henry Herrington operated the plant for another period of time. In September 1897, M.O. Leyda bought the Gold Spring Creamery and must have moved the machinery and equipment to Pattersonville, using it when he and John Rutledge built the creamery there.

The area railroad stations were not only for transporting goods and a stop-over for traveling from place to place; they were also a meeting place to share gossip or just simply relax. Many of the railroads were a source of transportation for area high school students. A southbound train would leave Bayard heading toward Minerva and would arrive with students at about 9:30 a.m. Irene Armstrong Schandel gave an account of the railroad:

> We had two trains a day. It helped us to get to High School. It brought our mail. We loaded carloads of hay at Hibbets; livestock buyers loaded livestock there. Saturday night trains may have been a Whiskey Special but we needed the service. The train stopped at Leyda's Crossing and Stemple's, if you flagged it.

Several of these little areas, such as Leyda's Crossing and Stemple's, were just stops for the railroad. Leyda was platted on February 17, 1837 by Henry Leyda in Brown Township. It served as a way station on the W&LE and had no commercial significance. Stemple was in Washington Township and also served as a way station for the W&LE. The Wathey's station, near Augusta, was named for the Wathey family, who lived in the area in 1818. Students from the area would catch the train here to attend Minerva High School. Local housewives took their produce to market in Minerva on this train. When the passenger service was discontinued in 1926, a self-contained unit was used, commonly known as "The Hoodle Bug."

Hibbets, which is believed to have been named for a family that lived in the area, was another way station when the railroad went through in 1853. On July 9, 1859, a post office was begun with George Harsh as the postmaster, although a March 31, 1882 newspaper account claims the post office did not open until that year and the postmaster was William Moser. Most likely at some point both of these men served the post office there. Mail service in Hibbets was discontinued on June 30, 1942.

Hibbets also had a general store, and in the spring of 1929, Agnes Benington purchased the land, which included the store, a house, and several other out buildings, from Hughes Gregory. This was a very daring thing for a woman, especially in the midst of the Depression, but her little country store handled general merchandise, groceries, dry goods, hardware, feed, and fertilizer. There was also gas sold for automobiles and kerosene for lamps. Many times, there was not enough money in the register to make change, but this did not matter. Customers still patronized her store. Trains ran two times a day then and there were usually a couple passenger cars and a couple freight cars running from Carrollton to Canton. Local farmers brought their milk to be loaded from a platform into the baggage car and taken to Windsor Evaporated Milk Products Company in Carrollton. Passengers could get on or off the train here.

In the rear of Benington's store was an old freight car that served as a freight house. Merchandise would be stored there until local citizens could pick up their

Later the site of Heritage Plastics, this was the Windsor Evaporated Milk plant in Carrollton where dairy products from Hibbets were delivered. (Courtesy Dick Griffin.)

This is an aerial view of Hibbets. The building in the lower left served as the train depot and grocery store. (Velma Griffin Collection.)

items. There was also a pot-bellied stove and benches where section hands could get out of the rain or cold, eat their lunches, or just warm up. At one time, the railroad officials gave orders for the building to be torn down, but Benington soon let them know that the building was essential for business; the officials ended up repairing and painting the building instead. During this time, there were a lot of "tramps" or "hobos" who traveled the rails and Benington would sometimes allow them to stay a night in the freight room, but only when she locked them in for the night. Benington was also known to make sandwiches of bologna and Swiss cheese between slices of bread with mustard or ketchup for the section hands, road workers, or whomever. She sold them for 35¢. Horseradish was also known to grow abundantly near the tracks and Benington would make mustard pickles with it.

Eventually, the train was cut to once a day, then twice a week, and then down to once a week. By that time, local people would fight to get a seat. Eventually, the train did not stop in Hibbets at all unless it was flagged down and now not even the buildings remain. Benington's youngest son Edgar remembered enough to give us this information through his wife Isabel in 1994.

The Hibbets post office carried mail to Kilgore when rural routes began. Kilgore's post office started with George Pugh in 1835. The postmaster was Joseph Parker. The mail was carried on horseback and when the postmaster approached, he blew a horn so Parker could come out and receive the mail. In

This image shows the train depot at Tabor Station. A portion of this building was removed to Petersburg and is now the Biscuit House for the Algonquin Mill Festival. (Velma Griffin Collection.)

"The largest little town in the U.S." is the building that held almost a dozen businesses. (Velma Griffin Collection.)

1904, the post office moved to the home of Mary J. Barr and later to the residence of Herbert J. Farber.

A better known railroad station was Scott's Station at Tabor. Once located along state route 39, Tabor was billed at the 1892 Chicago World's Fair as "The Largest Little Town in the U.S." because one building there housed 11 businesses. The railroad station called Scott's Station was named for W.C. Scott, who operated the nearby coal mines. Four trains came through daily bringing mail, merchandise, and visitors to the community. The area adopted the name Tabor because there was already a Scott's Station in Ohio. A post office was another business in this building.

The 24-by-36-foot frame building consisted of a storeroom, kitchen, and dining room with a pantry and bedroom on the first floor. There were four bedrooms on the second floor for a boardinghouse. This was also a drop point for wild horses shipped in from the West and sold for $40 per head to those brave enough to try to break them. Soon, a horse dealership and blacksmith shop were also located in this building. There was also a stockyard, general store, lumberyard, creamery drop, and telephone exchange here, followed by an oil distributorship.

The title at the World's Fair was a result of Winfield Shotwell and his brother-in-law Thomas Davis, who were traveling for the International Harvester Company in the late 1880s. The company representatives were so impressed with everything in one building that they decided to make it their company display at the World's Fair at the quad-centennial of Christopher Columbus's discovery in 1492. Tabor also hosted many Saturday night parties. Without much coaxing, George Bulger, an Englishman who worked in the local coal mines, would play his violin. He was said to have played for Queen Victoria before coming to the United States. He was supposedly so talented that he could lay down the bow and slide the violin strings up and down the stovepipe on the pot-bellied stove and still make beautiful music. The railroad to this portion of the county was discontinued in 1935 and 1936 when Atwood Lake was constructed.

The railroad did not bring the prosperity the people had hoped for, but it was still essential to the residents socially and culturally as a means for diversion and social interaction. In previous times, entertainment was on a local level: box and pie socials, fiddling, dancing, cakewalks, spelling bees, and taffy pulls. There were also ball games, picnics, sleigh riding, and wood carving. These things continued, but with the railroad, residents had a choice of which village they wanted to go to and participate in these events. It also widened their choices of events; now they could attend political, cultural, and social affairs, or just go to the cities to shop. The affairs of other villages were more accessible and often people would walk the tracks to avoid the muddy roads. Homes built during this period were designed to face the railroad tracks instead of the road.

In Leesville, residents would go to the train station on Sunday just to watch people arrive. Nearby Bowerston was home to Penn's Department Store, known as one of the largest department stores in the state at that time, and people would come from all over to shop there. Purchases could be taken directly to the train station and could be taken home the same day.

The only functioning railroad other than the Elderberry Excursion Line train is the Ohi-Rail Corporation, which operates the railroad between Minerva and Hopedale, from the depot and operating headquarters at Mechanicstown, on Ohio Route 39 in eastern Carroll County. Ohi-Rail shortline starts at Bayard and extends through the village of Minerva. It slices across Carroll County, passing through Pattersonville, Watheys, Specht, Mechanicstown, and Wattsville where the line enters Jefferson County at Bergholz and Amsterdam. From there, it continues into Harrison County, terminating at Hopedale where it joins with W&LE Pittsburgh-Brewster mainline. Ohi-Rail is a contract common-carrier operator that has been in business since July 30, 1982. It is one of the many small railroads known as shortlines that sprung up after Congress deregulated the United States rail industry in 1980. One of the purposes in establishing a shortline between Minerva and Hopedale was to maintain some rail access to the vast coal reserves of Jefferson and Harrison Counties. Ohi-Rail has not only survived through diversifying away from a total dependence on Ohio's high sulfur coals, but has gone through a 2.7-mile expansion between Minerva and Bayard. The line was initially opened in 1884 from Alliance/Minerva to the then new mines in the Bergholz area. The railroad ran right up to and against a big tree at the end of town. The Village of Bergholz, in fact, derived its name from the chief engineer for the construction of the railroad, Alliance resident W.R. Bergholz. Between

1884 and 1902, the line was further constructed south to a new mining camp where Amsterdam now exists. Finally, the line was completed another 23 miles into Hopedale.

The busiest years for this line were during World War II and between 1958 and 1964 when there were three major mines working: North American Coal Corporation's Jensie Deep Mine near East Springfield, Hanna Coal Company's Marion Mine near Hopedale (Cherry Valley), and Hanna Coal's Piney Fork Mine and Preparation Plant (West Farms strip and Friendship Park deep mine near Smithfield). Throughout this era and into the 1970s, the line hosted a half-dozen on again, off again strip mine tipple operations. The line's last haul was 1977, just prior to the implementation of the federal Clean Air Act, which ultimately displaced about 20 million annual tons of Ohio high-sulfur coal production from the market. Locally, the line dropped from hauling 4 million tons annually to almost none by 1982. The Ohi-Rail maintains a 1955 model engine that is capable of hauling ten loaded coal cars.

When Con-Rail abandoned its railroad lines on April 5, 1982, brothers Tom and John Barnett from Salineville, members of Ohi-Rail, became active in seeing the line purchased by the Ohio Transportation Authority. The line consists of the 34-mile Minerva to Hopedale spur, the Wolf Run Lead of 3.8 miles, and the Pekin Spur of 1.6 miles. Operation of the Minerva to Hopedale spur of Ohi-Rail began on July 30, 1982 and became official in September 1982. Summitville Tile in Pekin was the first industry served by the reactivated railroad. Two Minerva residents operate the train: Dave Unkefer serves as engineer and Tom Campbell as brakeman and conductor. The end of operations by Con Rail posed a definite hardship on area industries, and the establishment of the new company ensured the maintenance of outlets for the Minerva and Pekin industries. This line serves active coal mines in Jefferson and Carroll Counties, as well as the ceramic and paper industries in Minerva. Ohi-Rail is a subsidiary of Indiana Hi-Rail Corporation and runs through Carroll, Harrison, and Jefferson Counties.

Modern railroads were greatly advanced by Minerva resident Willard Pennock. Born on his father's farm near Augusta on July 21, 1852, Pennock joined E.M. Jerome and Arthur Hostetter in 1871 as the first graduating class of Minerva High School. In 1874, he formed a partnership with his brother Isaac in a manufacturing business in Minerva. In 1879, the Pennock brothers began manufacturing narrow gauge railroad cars in Minerva. Fire destroyed their original plant, but by 1882 they had organized the Minerva Car Works on the site of the former Minerva Wax Paper with the Pennock brothers as proprietors. From 1890 to 1896, William Pennock secured patents on his inventions of pressed steel cars and car trucks. With machines designed especially by him, Pennock built the first cars and trucks of this type to be used on American railways.

Communication was greatly opened between settlers and their friends and families in the east with the introduction of the railroad. Replacing the Pony Express, railroads carried mail from station to station and were a main reason many villages changed their names. Mail bags were hung out on flag stop standards and

This image shows the old train depot at Leesville. (Courtesy Dan Rees.)

an arm swung out from the train to catch the bag. Since it was popular to name a village for a former home, too many villages in the state or tri-state area had the same name. Thus, too much confusion was created for railroad stops and mail delivery, so new names were chosen. Cannonsburgh was changed to Dellroy, and Perrysville's post office became Lamartine, but the residents still called their home Perrysville.

Before the Lamartine post office was established, Jacob Gladden Sr. kept a post office on his farm and called it Hickory. This name was most likely for Andrew Jackson, who had many admirers in Perry Township. Hickory post office was visited once every two weeks and the chief mail was a few copies of the *Cadiz Sentinel* and the *Carrollton Picayune*, which were eagerly sought after. Hickory post office was abandoned when Lamartine was established on April 25, 1848 with Alexander Johnston as postmaster. This post office closed in 1954 when the rural routes were established, but the little village still remains as Perrysville.

The village of Leesburgh became Leesville as there were three Leesburghs in the area. The railroad and post office agreed to change the name, which they did by 1900—at least on the surface. It was never officially or legally changed on any documents and either name has been used, but not interchangeably. Mail carried to Petersburg was labeled Tope's Mill and placed in a box in Carrollton. The contents would be taken out by anyone who lived in that neighborhood and delivered to the mill for distribution. In 1903, rural mail routes were begun, and in 1913, parcel post began. Mail carried by rail served until 1970.

The first mail carried to Augusta was hauled from Kensington to Augusta by horses over extremely bad roads. There was a tri-weekly mail route from Carrollton to Kensington for several years during the 1800s. A contract for this route was let to Ellsworth Harsh on March 4, 1887, for four years. After the Cleveland, Youngstown & Pittsburgh Railroad was built, the mail was hauled from Augusta Station and continued in that manner until it was delivered by truck.

A post office was established in Pattersonville after the railroad was built. Mrs. Annie Cassidy was the first postmistress. The post office was discontinued on October 31, 1957 and the mail delivered by the rural carrier from Minerva.

Mail service in Malvern began in 1844. On December 21, 1918, the post office safe was blown open and the contents stolen. A good portion of money was likely stolen as the 1919 fiscal year reported having done a business of $2,291.01 and money orders in the amount of $35,000. In 1920, it became a third-class post office and had only one rural free delivery route with Robert W. Hewitt as its carrier. The postmaster received his commission in August 1919 and only had one office clerk, Ora B. McMillen.

Carrollton's post office was started in 1846 with Henry A. Stidger as postmaster. In 1851, Congress ordered the use of postage stamps and it was on May 25, 1853 that the first mail was delivered by the railroad. The Carrollton post office became second-class in 1921 with six rural routes. The carriers for

This building has been home to many things over the years. As shown here, it was once a car dealership. Now it is the Free Press Standard *offices. (Courtesy Dick Griffin.)*

those routes were James R. Hill, R.L. McFadden, Oriel C. Walsh, Oliver C. Scott, David Blazer, and John W. Maple. The two village carriers were A.A. Markley and A.L. Rainsberger. Carrollton post office was also victim to having its safe blown up. The first time was around 1917 and the second time around 1919, possibly due to the increase of War Savings stamps. During 1920, $335,000 worth was sold.

In 1879, the first telegraph line was strung along the railroad with Will J. Baxter as the first telegraph operator of the Carrollton station. The telegraph had been invented just prior to the Civil War. With the extension of the railroad came a network of telegraph lines, unifying the country and bringing the latest news to the newspapers and citizens of isolated areas. The news of the entire country, even the world, was now at their fingertips. As citizens became familiar with the issues, not only in their immediate area but in the whole country, their understanding and fervor for politics grew. Thus, many politicians and orators found it essential to speak in the opera houses and picnic groves of the villages and countryside. William McKinley spoke in 1900 at the Fourth of July picnic and celebration just north of Leesville.

This new way of receiving news also opened the door for many newspapers to begin, although printing was nothing new to the area. The first printing press was brought by John Swartzell of Pekin in 1816. He published *The Mormon Journal* for a short time. There were many newspapers published in Carroll County over the years, but most were short lived. Very little is known about most of these, except the date of their founding: *The Jeffersonian* (July 1837), the *Carroll Democrat* (June 3, 1843), *The Democratic Crisis* (April 12, 1844), the *Ohio Picayune* (July 16, 1846), *The New Era* (August 13, 1849), and *The Citizen Democrat* (January 1856).

Some of the small villages had newspapers also. A small weekly newspaper called *The Augusta Gazette* was published in Augusta in 1879 by William Roach, Adam Myers, and others. Leesville had a newspaper called *Conotton Valley Times*, published by M.C. Price. The *Malvern News* dates back to the *Minerva News and Clay City Times* in 1884, which was run by H.D. Williams and Son until 1918. It was the starting place of five other newspapers. The paper is printed in Minerva and now called simply the *Minerva News*. (The *Clay City Times* portion was published just for the citizens of Malvern.) Harlem Springs had a newspaper called *The Rural Tiara* that was established in 1845 by Fielding S. Cable. After just a few weeks he turned the plant over to Robert Craven and William Crow, who ran a $2,000 lottery along with their newspaper.

The first newspaper in Carrollton was the *Centreville Recorder* in 1832. It was a publication of Columbiana County and Volume 1, No. 1 is dated September 8, 1832. It was a weekly paper with a subscription rate of $2 a year. It had four pages of five columns each and no column rules. Joshua D. Patton was the editor and proprietor. In 1834, this paper merged with the *Gazette* and became the *Free Press*, published by Pearce and Christy.

In the winter of 1845 and 1846, the Ohio legislature passed a law providing for the filing of two newspapers of opposite politics in each county's auditor's office.

The first of these political papers was the *Carroll Chronicle*, which was established in March 1871 by 25 leading and wealthy democrats of Carroll County. It was printed on a hand press by J.V. Lawler, who was hired from the *Salem Republican*. Professor D.J. McAdams, the superintendent of Carrollton schools at that time, became the editor. He only served for a few months and was replaced by lawyer Thomas Hays, who divided his time between his law practice and the paper. By 1917, the *Carroll Chronicle* was being printed on a cylinder press and a steam engine and was eight pages, each composed of seven 22-inch columns. The *Carroll Republican* followed in 1881 and was published by Samuel J. Cameron until his death in 1894. The *Free Press* was bought in 1897 by the Kemmerer Brothers, who merged with the *Sherrodsville Standard* and became the *Free Press Standard*, which changed hands many times, but still operates as the only newspaper in Carrollton.

Rural Free Delivery mail routes extended connection with other people and other places. The company delivered mail to the major portion of the rural population and was largely appreciated. It was carried by horses or mules pulling a cart, buggy, or mail wagon. When the automobile was introduced, it replaced the mail wagons.

Just as the canals closed due to the railroad, the railroads faded when the automobile was introduced. The first automobile in Carrollton was brought by Frank Lowe of Steubenville. He arrived on August 10, 1900 and gave a ride to General Ephraim R. Eckley (aged 97) and Doctor John Moody (aged 98). Lowe had come to Carrollton to visit his aunts after traveling through New England and agreed to give the gentlemen a ride when they approached him. It was the first time either of the men had been in an automobile.

The railroad especially faded after World War I and the early 1920s when trucking became the norm for shipping goods. Unlike the canals, the railroads did not close completely; they just were not as popular. Goods were often shipped by train and truck. The introduction of paved roads focused on Carrollton. One of the first roads connected the Jefferson County Paving at Amsterdam and the Stark County Paving at Oneida. The road from Carrollton to the Stark County line paralleled the W&LE in 1916. The paving only extended a little over a mile north of Carrollton past the fairgrounds, and over a mile south into Union Township. To the east, it went about 2 miles toward Harlem Springs.

The roads in Malvern were first paved in 1915 at a cost of $35,000 and the pavements ran from 30 to 40 feet in width. These roads were made of local paving bricks.

Shortly before 1900, a poll tax was introduced. Each male citizen between the ages of 21 and 65 was assessed $3 a year with the privilege of working this out on the road at $1.50 a day, or the full $3 if he brought his team of horses and worked with them. Some men would put their team to a road grader with one or two others and make ditches along the sides of the road. Others would take their team and wagon and haul stone from a field to the road where others would break up the stone to fill in the holes in the road. Many stone fences were built along the road in this same manner. A road supervisor was appointed by the trustees and was always on the job to make sure everything went as planned.

Several years before, a law was passed that made it the duty of each board of township trustees to set aside $50 each year to build and maintain watering troughs along the public roads for the benefit of horses. In town, the roads were maintained by the local men. Once a year, the men would come with rakes, hoes, and other instruments that would aid in restoring the dirt roads to a smoother surface.

Some of the first "paved" roads were made of broken pieces of pottery. The main road through Perrysville that ran from Carrollton to New Hagerstown was one of these roads and the pottery came from the Carrollton and Scio potteries. In 1937, the road was replaced with State Route 332.

About the same time paved roads were introduced, the telephone was introduced. The Bergholz Telephone Company started in 1900. At that time, a few progressive citizens of Mooretown constructed a line connecting James George's store with the Bergholz depot. In April 1902, the Bergholz Telephone Company was organized and lines were constructed to connect Bergholz, Amsterdam, East Springfield, and Salineville. Long distance service was established through East Springfield to Steubenville and through Salineville to exchanges of the United States Telephone Company lines. In June, the company was incorporated by W.E. and L.W. Steinmetz, A.G. and James McBane, and Dr. J.W. and S.G. Carson, and a switchboard was installed in the residence of A.G. McBane in Bergholz.

Driving is Frank Lowe with General Ephraim Eckley and Doctor John Moody in the back seat. (Courtesy George Rankin.)

The telephone did not come into use as quickly as the telegraph as voices did not transmit as easily as sound. Augusta Township was first with an experimental line. They hooked up with the Bergholz Company, and when it worked, the Eastern Ohio Company built a main line from East Rochester, Ohio to Augusta, then branched out from this line. Each subscriber was charged $1 a month. The Farmer's Line was also organized, headquartered in Pattersonville, about the same time, by a group of local citizens for the purpose of getting telephone service to as many residents as possible. The lines from Pattersonville extend to cover a part of four townships. The telephone company was sold to L.D. Wilson in August 1937. This family operated it for many years, and in 1962, changed the lines to the dial system. The name was then changed to Pattersonville Telephone Company.

The first telephone exchange was at W.G. Donaldson's store in Scroggsfield. Shortly after the Bergholz Telephone Company was established, the Scroggsfield exchange was laid. It connected W.G. Donaldson's store to the Wattsville Depot. The work was completed and phones installed. The success of this enterprise was a surprise to many doubters and surpassed everyone's expectations. As a result, R.A. McLaughlin, W.G. Donaldson, James George, and Ernest Favri organized the Scroggsfield Telephone Company, connecting the homes of several farmers, and installed a switching station in W.G. Donaldson's store with Donaldson as operator. By April 1902, the company had 27 subscribers and the business increased so rapidly that Donaldson, with his large mercantile business, was unable to devote the necessary time to the telephone affairs. An exchange was then opened in the home of Sadie J. Andrews in Scroggsfield, with Andrews as operator. The Scroggsfield Telephone Company's lack of long distance

This is an early 1900s photo of the men coming out to repair Main Street in Carrollton taken from the square looking west. (Courtesy George Rankin.)

connections appealed to the Bell Telephone Company, but they were unable to agree upon terms that would be fair to the small company. Instead, a line was built to Bergholz and arrangements were made for the consolidation of the two independent companies.

The merger took place in November 1902 under the name of the Bergholz Telephone Company with R.A. McLaughlin as general manager. Soon after, a line was constructed to Carrollton. McLaughlin and his wife moved to Carrollton in 1904 and their daughter Grace was placed in charge of the exchange. By the mid-1900s, most of the county was covered with telephone lines. The Crescent Telephone Company came into the Sherrodsville area around 1903.

When the telephone reached Perrysville, the office was in Bob Henry's house. At first, around 1915, you could talk to Scio by switchboard. By 1921, you could talk to Carrollton. The switchboard operator was Lilly Gotschall. The telephone office was closed in 1930 and moved to Carrollton. The first telephone in a private home was in 1938 in the home of William Barnhouse, who owned the grocery store in the area.

Alexander Graham Bell may have invented the telephone, but the "Father of the Bell Telephone System" was Theodore Newton Vail, who was born in Brown Township. His father Lewis Vail and Joseph Tidbald received a land grant of 145 acres from the General Land Office of the United States on December 1, 1829 and began at once to clear the land that is now Malvern. On July 16, 1845, Theodore Vail was born in a small frame house on the corner of Reed and Porter Streets. When he was two years old, the family moved to Morristown, New Jersey. At the age of 16, he entered Morristown Academy and studied chemistry, astronomy, and natural philosophy. When he graduated, he could not decide what he wanted to do, so he took a job as a drug clerk in Smith's Drug Store in Morristown.

At the time, the American Magnetic Telegraph was in operation in this drugstore. Vail soon learned to read messages by sound instead of the tape method used. Two years later, in 1864, he was employed by the Western Union Telegraph Company as an operator in New York. Later, he moved to Iowa and worked as an operator for the Union Pacific Railroad. While working there, he devised a system for sorting and distributing mail. Postal authorities in Washington heard of his innovations and made him General Superintendent of the Railway Mails. Vail became very discouraged with trying to teach his technique to others, so he returned to communications and bought stock in the newly-created Bell Company. The company had no capital to construct a general telephone system, so they had to promote local companies in the towns that in turn would pay the company a certain percentage of their profit for the use of the franchise and rental of their instruments. Vail's idea was to have one company, one policy of operation, but universal service.

In 1878, Bell's father-in-law brought Vail into the company as general manager. There was a long court fight over who had actually invented the telephone and when Western Union conceded and agreed it was Bell, they agreed to let Bell handle local companies, while they would take care of long distance. Vail fought this arrangement until finally Western Union and Vail agreed on a deal to add over 56,000 telephones to 55 cities with Bell's outreach. Bell also agreed not to enter the telegraph business. The Bell Telephone Company was established and became a financial success through Vail's untiring efforts. Shortly after the company changed its name to American Telephone and Telegraph Company in 1887, Vail retired. The Vail home in Malvern was recognized in July 15, 1945 by the N.C. Kingsbury Chapter, Telephone Pioneers with a bronze tablet on the Porter Street side of the house. Alexander G. Bell invented the telephone, but Vail made it a business.

The introduction of the automobile brought with it much excitement and grief. An Augusta Township citizen was known for riding the first motorcycle in to Toledo, Ohio. His name was Johnson Crawford and the cycle was made in Paris. The police arrested him, but could not find anything in the books to fine him for. Instead, they requested he take them each for a ride to show them what the machine could do.

Another major source of transportation in Carroll County was the establishment of the airport. Known as Tolson Field, it was dedicated on October 8, 1967 with Governor James A. Rhodes cutting the ribbon. The need for an airport was first recognized in 1946 when a small one was established. The expansion of that facility was noted by a number of progressive citizens of the county, and early in 1965, the county commissioners appointed a committee to study the feasibility of a county airport. The project qualified for state assistance under Governor Rhodes's program to assist every county wanting an airport to have one. Hundreds of Carroll County residents dug in to meet the requirements necessary to develop the facility by contributing not only cash, but time, labor, and equipment. By the time of the dedication, the airport consisted of 67 acres with a 4,300-foot, asphalt northeast-southwest runway and a nearly new brick building, formerly a home, which was converted into an administration building and restaurant. A locally owned charter service was established in 1973 to serve the needs of the community.

The name Tolson Field was in honor of Mr. and Mrs. Melvin Tolson, who made the initial donation of land for the port. Today, Tolson Field houses 21 aircraft; only one is a multi-engine airplane. Seventy-five percent of the general aviation is local with 23 percent transient. Of the other 2 percent, one is air taxi and the other military. The airport also has a grass strip 1,600 feet by 85 feet that is usable for takeoff and landing if necessary. Officials warn users to be careful of deer on and near the air strip. The airport celebrated its 35th anniversary in October 2002.

5. Reading, Writing, and Arithmetic

Being hearty and courageous people, once the settlers had established their homes, they began working together for the improvement of their communities. Their first concern was for the education of their children. Schools and the provision for them began before there was a United States settlement northeast of the Ohio River. The school lands were granted to the state in 1803. Congress reserved section 16 of each township for public schools. This section was generally near the center of the township. Quite often, students had to walk a great distance to attend school and parents worried for their safety. Another stipulation at that time was that before and after the land grants provided any income, existing schools were to be sustained wholly or principally by private subscription, meaning that only the children whose parents could afford to employ a teacher could attend school. All the bills were paid by the parents of the children attending the school. A teacher would require a minimum of 20 pupils and would be paid for six days a week, eight hours a day, at the rate of $1 to $2 per pupil for the term. Half of this tuition was paid in money, the other half in wheat. This may seem like a low payment, but only a small percentage of parents could afford it. If there were several children in the family, they often did not receive much of an education; therefore, most children could not read or write.

Most were one-room log schoolhouses. The first was in Lee Township near Millensburgh. Another early school was in Brown Township and was presided over by Edward Milner. A third was in Leesburgh and was taught by Thomas Butterfield. John D. Patterson, a resident near Pattersonville, built a schoolhouse on his own farm and taught a three-month-term private school and received $13 in wages. Augusta Township in what was then Columbiana County had a school called the "Friends" School House and is the earliest known school in that area. The schoolmaster was Nathan Pim, who passed away in 1816 and was laid to rest near the school. The building was later sold to the Quaker church and Pim is believed to be the first person buried in its cemetery.

These log schoolhouses generally measured 16 by 18 feet square and the joists were so low that larger students could grab them and swing to and fro. The only light came through greased paper fastened over openings cut in each side of the school. There was a fireplace just 4 feet inside the door with a crudely made chimney.

The schoolmasters of the day were as a rule, elderly, crippled, or males who were unable to do manual labor. Teaching was regarded as a very light occupation. If a healthy young man applied for the job, he was considered lazy. Parents took turns providing room and board for the teachers. When teachers could not be found, qualified fathers took over, but not to the detriment of the farm.

When it came to discipline of the students, a rod or switch was used from a nearby birch tree. Sometimes teachers would use a ruler to simply strike the hand of the disobedient child. Students were much more in control and morality was not an issue. The Bible was used as a textbook, along with the *American Primer*, *Dilworth's Spelling Book*, and *Walsh's Arithmetic*. Grammar and geography were considered unnecessary and rarely taught. Courses in philosophy, physiology, chemistry, music, and art were unheard of as anything more than extracurricular activities. Slates provided the principal writing surface, and if paper was available, it was very coarse. The ink was made from maple bark or poke berries. In spite of a lack of teaching equipment, students were very well educated, even by today's standards.

Sessions were held in late fall (winter session) and in spring (summer session) for three months each. Many students dropped out to work on family farms, especially after learning the traditional three R's in the fourth grade. The spring term was often taught by a woman and generally the only students there were the small children and girls.

In 1821, the first law was passed authorizing the levying of tax to support the schools. This law allowed all children an opportunity to learn. Parents no longer had to pay for the education of their children. The law also provided that each township be divided into school districts and that funds be raised to build schoolhouses. Then, in 1852, a stronger and better working law was passed that ordered the county commissioner to levy a tax on all property to be used for a school fund; thus began real estate taxes.

Four years later, it became mandatory for teachers to be examined before they could be employed. Until 1838, this exam only covered the three R's. With the tax support, schools became more available to more children. There were usually several schools in each township and they were administered by a board of directors elected by popular vote. With funds for building schools, the old log schoolhouses were soon replaced by frame, brick, or stone structures. These buildings not only provided education to the schoolchildren, but gave citizens a place to hold social gatherings.

The first school in Malvern was built around 1835 or 1836 and is still standing at 214 Porter Street. Sometime before 1876, it was remodeled as a home and was only recently discovered to have been the school.

Reverend Samuel Martin and Reverend W.H. Buchanan taught in the McCook building over George J. Butler's store. James Gallagher taught in the old jail.

The names of these students from the Malvern School No. 1 are unknown. (Courtesy Carroll County Historical Society.)

In 1845, Carrollton was divided into three school districts: the Canal Street schoolhouse, the Sheep Hill schoolhouse, and the Lisbon street schoolhouse, on the comer of North Lisbon and Grant Streets (now the corner of North Lisbon and Fifth Streets). All the sub-district schoolhouses were built of brick by William and George Woodward.

In 1867, Carrollton's three one-room schools were combined and a large brick school called Union School was built, sufficient for the entire town at that time with grades one through twelve. It cost $12,000 to build; $450 went to Jacob Helfrich for the lot and $10 went to Gus Rothacker for drawing the plans. William Bricker did the woodwork, Rue & Wetzel of Minerva did the brickwork, and George Hemming did the stonework. T.H. Atkinson roofed the building.

Three years before the school was built, a special assessment was made and the building was paid for without a bond issue. Three rooms were opened before the building was plastered and the first teachers were Sade McLaughlin, Lizzie Lawler, and David Fryer. Professor J.D. McAdams was the first superintendent. The board consisted of Jacob Helfrich, Elisha McGuire, and Joseph Carnahan. The Union School's first commencement was Friday, June 27, 1879 in the school auditorium. The graduates were Mattie Atkinson, Maggie Rukenbrod, Lillian McCoy, and Flora Mortland.

Carrollton's school board was among the first in the state to comply with the law requiring doors to swing outward, and at the same time, the stairway was

Two of Augusta's early school buildings were most likely built in the mid-1800s. These buildings were removed when all students were consolidated into the 1927 building.

changed—two stairways were constructed to carry out the provisions of the law governing school buildings. The building originally consisted of six rooms and a large hall; the latter was used as a skating rink, opera house, and ballroom. Later, the hall was converted into two rooms to accommodate the growing demands.

When the county system of schools was by districts, there were usually three directors from each township and six to eight districts in each township. Under this system, Augusta Township had the following districts. Number 1 was Stonepile, which was a stone schoolhouse built by William Kennedy, a stone mason and farmer living in that district. Early records show that Edwin Ferrall taught schoolhouse Number 3, located on the west side of County Road 10, approximately 200 yards south of where Township Road 269 joins County Road 10. In the winter of 1841 and 1842, daily attendance was 45 students. At that time, wages were $10 to $15 a month and board was around $1 a week.

District Number 2 was known as Dewey Hall District and had four schools. The fourth schoolhouse was built about 1896, the same time Admiral George Dewey was made a hero by destroying the Spanish fleet in Manila Bay without losing a man. The board decided to change the name of the school district to Dewey Hall in honor of Admiral Dewey. After its closing in the 1930s, school Number 4 was moved and rebuilt into a dwelling southeast of Carrollton at the junction of state Routes 9 and 43. Number 3 was formerly known as Whole Bark School. The ground for the school was on Whole Bark Creek and was donated by Mr. and Mrs. Beatty about 1830. The name came from a tannery located at the head of the valley that used the whole bark of the trees instead of the customary procedure of grinding it to use for the tanning of the hides in making leather.

The first building was made of logs; the second of frame. It was not plastered and the blackboard consisted of two wide boards fastened together and painted black. Sometime after 1884, this was replaced with a third building with plastered walls and a slate blackboard. The first frame building was moved to Pattersonville, where it was first used to store wool by John Burtsfield and later converted into a dwelling with a storeroom in the front by Harry McLain. It was known for many years as Pattersonville Post Office and Henry's General Store. Since Henry's retirement in 1964, both the post office and store have been closed. The second frame school was purchased by J. Howard Mangun in 1939. Mangun moved it several hundred feet west of its original location and remodeled it into a dwelling.

District Number 4 was called Muddy Fork, being near the end of Lower Muddy Fork Valley. It had two known schoolhouses. The first school was located on the east side of the road on the farm originally settled by the James Moreledge family. Near the first schoolhouse was a dam and old mill pond used for a sawmill. The children often skated there in winter. The second building was located on the opposite side of the road where township Road 251 converges with County Road 43. It replaced the first building on the farm then owned by the Moreledge and Francis Jackson families. This district was transferred to the Minerva School District about 1930. The building was torn down and moved to Louisville to be rebuilt into a dwelling.

Number 5 was called Enterprise and it had three schoolhouses. The first one is said to have been built in 1839. A third school was built in 1892 by John L. Smith, a carpenter from Augusta, and replaced the second frame schoolhouse. It was purchased by Robert Noling in 1936 and made into a dwelling.

Eureka, from the Greek word meaning "I have found it," was District Number 6. It also had three schoolhouses. The first school was a stone building, located a half-mile northwest of the others and used as a school in the 1850s and 1860s. The second was replaced by the third schoolhouse, built in 1899 also by John L. Smith. The last one built in this district was moved to the farm of E.A. Imhoff in the 1930s, about 1 mile east of State Route 9, and made into a dwelling.

The seventh and final district was the Augusta district. The first school is said to have been built in 1833 on the north side of Augusta. It was rebuilt in 1853 as a two-story, two-room brick building that burned in 1924. In 1887, the board of education appropriated $1,600 for a new school, as it had been holding Select Schools at times and needed more room. After quite a controversy, the contract was given to John Hyatt, a local carpenter, to build a two-room, one-story frame building, which was completed in 1888. The lower grades occupied one room and the upper grades the other. About the year 1916, the first high school was started. It was a three-year high school, so students had to finish the fourth year elsewhere. About 1925, it became a four-year high school.

The present Augusta Township School building was built in 1927. Before it was completely finished, the old frame school burned. After the fire, the high school and what they could fit of the elementary students were moved into the new building. The rest of the students went to the township building. Being a four-year high school, East Township in Carroll County and Hanover Township in Columbiana County transported the majority of their high school students to Augusta by bus for several years, until they built a new high school of their own.

In the early 1930s, the schools of Augusta Township were centralized. The pupils from the rural districts of the township were brought into Augusta by bus. The township building was expanded and housed all grades. On November 15, 1965, the Augusta Board of Education passed a resolution to transfer all township assets and liabilities, and property, both real and personal, to the Carrollton Exempted Village Board of Education. The transfer to be consummated at noon on January 1, 1966. Augusta now houses students in preschool through sixth grade; grades seven through twelve attend Carrollton.

An article in the *Carroll Journal* on July 9, 1880 reported that the people of Mechanicstown had raised the funds to buy a lot and build a house "for use as a Mechanicstown Academy." It was intended for the building to be ready for the fall or winter term. Apparently, nothing more ever came of this school. It was the same in Augusta. The *Carroll Chronicle* of September 30, 1898 reported that funds were being raised to build a college in Augusta. It also reported that many individuals were trying to prevent it. Apparently they succeeded, as no college ever surfaced, although there was a select school there for a while. Another article in the *Carroll Chronicle*, dated March 22, 1878, announced to the public that a Professor T.B. Sawvel had been hired as principal of the Augusta Select School. They taught

This image shows a one-room school in Mechanicstown. The names of these students and their teacher have unfortunately been forgotten. (Courtesy Dan Rees.)

The New Harrisburg School right after it was completed. It is now an apartment building. (Courtesy Dan Rees.)

general studies, as well as natural science, literature, history, English etymology, and the method of teaching in preparation of actual teaching. There were also departments in music (vocal and instrumental), piano, organ, and violin. Tuition for a term of 12 weeks was $8. For instrumental music alone, with one lesson per week, the cost was $6. Boarding for ladies was $2 and $2.50 for men.

Until 1882, the schools of Harrison Township were supported by money rising from the rent of school section Number 16. After years of experiencing difficulties throughout the township, the school lands were sold on April 15, 1882. The popular vote on that issue was 120 for and 35 against. The New Harrisburg School in this township was built in 1931 as a combined grade and high school. Funds came from a bond issue voted for in the November 1930 election in the amount of $17,000. A newspaper account says, "The proposal reportedly received voter approval by a vote of 136 to 106 after a hot and bitter fight." For the first few years, there was no money to pay the teachers, yet they taught anyway. Dances were held in the gymnasium to help pay for the sidewalks. In 1960, New Harrisburg closed as a public school, and in 1968, the building was sold to the Carroll Hills Training Center for mentally and developmentally handicapped children.

Little is recalled of the Lee Township schools. They were Frog Hollow, Pleasant Hill, Strawcamp, Dutch Corner, Chestnut Grove, Number 8, Harlem Springs, and Highland Hall. Number 8 schoolhouse was built in 1840 and continued until 1922. The Harlem Springs Grade School was originally built in 1932, but burned the same year and had to be rebuilt in 1935. It began as a four-room school, housing grades one through eight with two grades in each room. Students in the higher grades were then bussed to Carrollton for a high school education. Until 1944, water had to be obtained from a hand pump outside the rear of the building. Indoor restrooms were installed in 1946. The school had its own gas pump on

Kilgore School, built in 1905, is the oldest school still used in the Carrollton Exempted Village School District. (Courtesy Jean Scarlott.)

the property for filling busses. As there was no playground equipment, students were allowed to bring their own sleds and toys to be used at recess. Two more classrooms and a cafeteria were added to the building in 1948. In 1960, Harlem Springs School became part of the Carrollton Exempted Village Schools. The 1935 building now houses kindergarten through third grade; the fourth through sixth grades attend Kilgore and eighth through twelve attend Carrollton.

Kilgore's first school was a one-room log building with a permanent desk around three sides of the room. The students sat on slab benches. This school stood on the ground below the current Methodist church. The present building was constructed in 1905 with Professor James Mills as principal. It was a third-class high school and stopped housing high school students for the 1948–1849 school year. Instead, students were bussed to Carrollton. Howard Johnson recalls he and ten of his classmates were very excited to have the chance to play football for the Carrollton team when this transfer was made. It was also at this time that the Carrollton team was no longer called the Black-n-Whites. The name "Warriors" was adopted and black and white became the school colors. This is still the tradition today.

Dellroy's first single-frame school was on Ginger Hill (now Ohio Street) and was replaced with two identical frame structures that served until 1893. A brick building was erected to serve as a two-year high school and elementary. It was classified as a third-grade school, which meant that a two-year program was provided. Due to curriculum changes, there was no graduating class in 1906. The Dellroy School became a second-grade school in 1916 with freshmen, juniors, and seniors. It became a first-class school in 1923 and the members of the class of 1922 graduated again in 1923 because a higher level of education was now available, and the original diplomas of the 1922 class were not valid. In that same year, a separate high school was constructed across the road and the former building was left for the elementary.

Students moved into the new building in 1925. The gymnasium had a dirt floor and the stage was a raised platform on the end of the it. A wooden floor was finally constructed in 1928. It was the early 1930s before the stage was moved to its current location. Hot lunches for these schools were provided by the PTA members. It was often soup made in the homes of each member and then warmed on oil stoves in the school. The elementary students were moved to the north side of the road in 1959 and the original building sat empty until 1974 when it was demolished. The site became the Monroe Township Park. The school system became a part of the Carrollton District in 1955. The school remained an elementary and junior high until 1968. Today, the brick high school serves as Dellroy Elementary and houses kindergarten through sixth grade with the remaining grades going to Carrollton.

While still using the district system, Glendale School was a building on the hillside along the east side of Glendale Hill (now Cactus Road). It closed in 1919

This school was razed when a new building was constructed across the road and is now the site of the Monroe Township park in Dellroy. (Velma Griffin Collection.)

and part of the building was removed to Dellroy where it was reassembled behind the present school. For years, it was used as an industrial arts classroom, but has since been torn down.

The Village of Atwood School is still standing on the water's edge of Atwood Lake. It once overlooked the railroad tracks, Indian Fork Creek, and the Atwood Store. Now it is a summer cottage still on its original site.

Perry Township's first school sat on what is now the corner of State Route 332 and State Route 164. The site is now the home of Gib Burton. The author's grandparents met at this school. There were no roads to get to the school at that time, only paths. Later, grades 1 through 6 were moved to the property now owned by Mr. and Mrs. Lee McIntosh. Grades 1 and 2 were in the building that is now their home. Grades 3 and 4 were in the front house and grades 5 and 6 were in the building that became Mary Scott's house.

In 1921, county superintendent D.L. Buchanan established a high school in Perrysville in the township hall. They had a girl's basketball team, with the court on the township building floor. Many school recitals were held in the hall as well. The first commencement was in 1924 with three graduates: Byron Shotwell, Georgia Hendricks, and Mildred Tope. The brick school building was constructed

This picture of the Perrysville Basketball team was taken c. 1964. Known as the Indians, most of these "boys" still reside in Carroll County.

A Union Township School now sits at the Algonquin Mill in Petersburg. (Velma Griffin Collection.)

in 1927 and sits on the property adjoining the McIntosh property. In 1934, the six grade schools throughout the township consolidated, and in September 1951, the high school students were sent to Scio. Perry Local School District closed on December 31, 1967 when it was made part of Carrollton District the following day. The building remained an elementary school (grades 1 through 6) until 1971 when all students were then sent to Carrollton. The school then closed and has changed hands many times since.

Rose Township had several one-room schools. One was located on the north side of Township Road 447 near Union Valley Church. It stood on property now owned by Smith Nursery of Magnolia. One of the former teachers of this school was one of the first to wear rubber-soled shoes and was known for being able to sneak up on the boys. Another Rose Township school was Number 2, located some distance from the secondary road. In bad weather, it was inaccessible by automobile. Former teacher Ruth Huffman Starlin would travel by horse and buggy to a nearby farm and continue on foot to the school with the children in these conditions. She worked eight months out of the year and earned $800. This school closed in 1933.

Woodsview School or Rose Township School Number 4 was near the junction of Township Road 147 and State Route 542. This school had a two-burner oil stove that was used to prepare hot lunches for the students. It closed in the early 1930s and was removed to the Glenn King property. The building was being used as a garage and storage in 1978.

Union Township was divided into six districts. The buildings were frame structures with benches around the walls for the students to sit on. When the

The Union School building in Carrollton is now the site of Carrollton Elementary School. (Courtesy George Rankin.)

weather was cold, students would gather around the fireplace and roast on one side while they froze on the other. At the noon hour, the boys helped get wood for the fireplace. The first school was a half-mile north of Petersburg. Later, a tract of land was purchased from Charles Crouse and a larger one-room school was built. Two rooms were added to it, but it was eventually abandoned because of centralization. Samuel Allward was the first teacher of Petersburg school. The second school in Union Township was Fawcett School, built on land from the Fawcett farm. Another school in Union Township was North Union School. One winter it had 60 students and the little ones had to sit three to a seat. This school had a literary society and housed the Sunday school in the summer. The other three schools in Union Township were Toot, Dutch, and McHugh.

Oak Grove School in Washington Township was closed about 1934 and the last teacher was Bertha Magee. The school building was sold in 1949 to Lloyd Nichols and it was moved to his property on State Route 39.

The only school now in Fox Township is Willis School, named for Victor B. Willis, who donated the land. It was dedicated on November 14, 1951. The cornerstone was laid in August 1950. It was a four-room brick structure that housed the consolidated schools of Number 16 and Mechanicstown. Guy Johnston of Steubenville was the contractor. At that time, Willis School was part of the Carroll County School system. It later became part of the Carrollton Exempted Village Schools. The building has since been expanded.

One-room schools in Fox Township included Number 16 and Mechanicstown, which were two buildings each with only one room. One building housed grades one through four and the other grades five through eight. Another one-room school sat above Wattsville, and Potts School was just south of Riley's church. It was in this schoolyard that John H. Morgan's men camped the night before their raid. The Greenbrier School is now Greenbrier Church near Salineville.

Leesville built a new school on north Union Street in 1906. The first floor was elementary and the second floor was high school. Students coming here from New Hagerstown were brought by horse and buggy. Most of the high school students walked. The first graduating class was in 1907 with two graduates. Later, this school only offered two years of high school and students had to go to another school—usually Bowerston or Sherrodsville—to graduate. This continued until the schools consolidated in 1949. In 1953, the Conotton Valley High School was constructed at a cost of $425,000. Dedicated in May 1953, it was not occupied by students until April 1, 1954. Students in grades seven through twelve from Leesville, Sherrodsville, Bowerston, and the neighboring vicinity still attend this school. The elementary students attend either Bowerston or Sherrodsville. Other schools in the early days of this area were Smiths, Leavittsville Road, Barricks Crossing, and Milltown. The Leesville grade school was closed in 1963.

Sherrodsville School was a first grade school only until it was granted a charter for second grade through high school in 1928. R.P. King was the superintendent,

The Union School in Carrollton is shown here being razed after it was declared unsafe. (Courtesy Dick Griffin.)

and in 1929, Charles Wells was head of the school. One year later, two rooms and an auditorium were added and the school received a first grade high school charter. Nine students received diplomas in 1931. This school later consolidated with Bowerston and formed Conotton Valley.

When the Union School in Carrollton was declared unsafe for use and it needed more classroom space, it was decided by a vote of 350 to 132 in the November 12, 1912 election to issue $50,000 in bonds to erect a new schoolhouse. The bonds were sold on December 14 to the Cummings Trust Company, and the contract was awarded to E.E. Bope of Columbus on January 13, 1913 on his bid of $47,125. After many changes and additions, the final cost was $75,000. Work on the building began in March 1913 on the site of the Union School, and while it was being constructed, the students were housed in the Methodist, Presbyterian, and United Presbyterian churches. The two primary rooms remained in the carriage shop, which had been redesigned for school purposes when the old building became too crowded. The next year, when the building was not ready in September as planned, all the students were housed in the Tabernacle. By the following September, all the setbacks were resolved and the new building was opened; however, it was not completed until December 1914. This building now houses the Carrollton Exempted Village School, grades two through six. Grades seven and eight are in the Bell-Herron Middle School, and all students from the outlying schools and in Carrollton, grades nine through twelve, attend the high school.

According to the superintendent's report of 1920, there were 88 one-room schools in use. These were staffed by 35 male teachers and 74 female. Pupils

Originally built as a high school, this is now the Bell-Herron Middle School, named for two former educators in the district.

totaled 2,063. When the district system was no longer used, George E. Bell of Guernsey County became the first county superintendent of schools. He assumed his duties on July 18, 1914. After Bell, on August 1, 1926, D.L. Buchanan became superintendent, remaining until December 15, 1931.

It was during Buchanan's term as superintendent that the general trend toward consolidation was begun by the State Department of Education. Consolidation of schools began. The last one-room school was in Norristown and it closed in 1952. One-room schools saw a drastic reduction, partly due to the adoption of the Ohio Elementary School Standards, which required schools to have at least three full-time teachers with no more than two grades housed in each classroom. Most of the one-room school buildings were torn down or moved. Some were converted into dwellings. Since the closing of the last one-room school, the students were absorbed into Carrollton Exempted Village School District. Other schools servicing students from Carroll County include Malvern, Minerva, Sandy Valley, Edison Local, Conotton Valley, Springfield Local, and Union Local.

At one time, there were two parochial schools, which were administered by the Steubenville Diocese of the Roman Catholic Church: Our Lady of Fatima School, an elementary school operated by the Sisters of Our Lady; and St. Edward's Central Catholic Junior-Senior High School, which taught seventh through twelfth grades. The beginnings of these schools were in 1950 when the Diocese of Steubenville offered a portion of the 84 acres owned by the church to Mother Clare and the Sisters of Charity in Caldwell, Ohio, whose facility had been condemned. The Carrollton facility was named St. John's Villa and opened its doors in June 1951 to dependent and neglected children aged two to fifteen. They rapidly outgrew the first building and a second was added in 1958. In the 1960s, when social reform advanced in the method of care for the homeless, orphans, and troubled youth, the Sisters changed the apostolate to reflect the new needs. A major emphasis was placed on educating the youth termed mentally handicapped or developmentally disabled. Our Lady of Fatima School and St. Edward's Central Catholic Junior-Senior High School were closed in the 1980s. St. John's Villa has also been home to the Growing Tree preschool since 1993, which was operated in their facility on Moody Avenue until November 1, 2002. On that date, the school, restaurant, and other facilities were moved to a new building on Crest Street.

Carroll County was also home to several colleges. One of the best known in the area was the Harlem Springs College, established in the fall of 1856 as a select school and begun by Professor Alfred D. Lee. For two years, William McCoy conducted this school as Harlem Springs Academy. In the fall of 1858, McCoy moved to Carrollton and opened a school there known as Centreville Academy. During this time Lee had been in Meadville, Pennsylvania attending Allegheny College. When Lee returned to Carroll County, he established a new school known as the Rural Seminary, approximately a mile from the springs of mineral water. To house the new school, he erected a two-story frame building with the addition of a tower in front at a cost of $3,000. The first term of the new seminary started on August 17, 1859. The school was coeducational from the start, but as a result of the Civil War and the drop in enrollment of young men, the Rural Seminary seemed to operate primarily as a female school during the war years. By the end of the Civil War, men were in attendance and outnumbered the ladies three to one. There were approximately 200 students by that time. Most were from the immediate vicinity; only a dozen were from out of state. The faculty was composed of five professors and three instructors in music: Alfred D. Lee, president and professor of natural and mental sciences; the Reverend Robert S. Hogue, professor of languages and moral science; Robert H. Howey, professor of mathematics and elocution; Amelia Lindsay, teacher of painting, drawing, German, and French; Mary J. Clark, assistant teacher in English branches; and Mary A. Hermon, Mary R. Magee, and Florence Emerson, teachers of music.

The 1866–1867 school catalog contained an announcement about the transfer of the seminary from Harlem Springs to New Market (later called Scio), 12 miles away. It was pointed out that the growth of the seminary made it necessary to enlarge the buildings. Any expansion, however, had to be made in view of the fact that Harlem Springs was 12 miles from the main line of any railroad and stagecoaches were reluctantly tolerated. Though there was space in Harlem Springs, this distance from the main lines of travel made Professor Lee decide to leave Harlem Springs and establish Scio College in Scho, Ohio. (After the closing of this college, it became a branch of Mount Union College in Alliance, Ohio.)

On November 23, 1867, Professor Robert Howey established a new school at Harlem Springs. He re-chartered it as Harlem Springs College. Seven years later, the buildings were destroyed by fire. A new building was constructed on the same site by the stockholders, with some aid from generous citizens. Professor Howey left the school in charge of Reverend S.L. Dickey in 1871. After some years, the student attendance dwindled and the school was closed. Mr. and Mrs. W.H. Shepherd opened a summer resort there that they conducted for two years, which was followed by the Harlem Springs public schools. In 1896, Professors J.L. Tope and Elmer Harsh opened an academy that continued for two years and again the public schools took over. In 1909, the property was purchased from Miss Sadie McLaughlin by Reverend C.W. Milan, pastor of the Methodist Episcopal church. The building was repaired and a college started that lasted for four years. Reverend Milan sold the property to William Dunlap of Harlem Springs and the college was reopened by Professor and Mrs. Ackerman. The enrollment fell off again and it was closed.

A hotel was then operated for three years by Mr. and Mrs. C.E. Thomas. Reverend Neibarger, a United Brethren minister, then took charge, conducting a one-week camp meeting in which all the churches joined. On September 4, 1924, the property was purchased by Edward D. and Herman D. Myers. The building was leased by Charles Johnson, who operated it as a hotel and summer resort known as the College Inn. Harry Robb leased the property and ran the College Inn similarly. On October 2, 1930, the college building was totally destroyed by fire. On May 15, 1942, Mr. and Mrs. Harry L. Toot purchased the property. At

The Harlem Springs College is shown here during the Civil War years. Notice there are only young ladies in this picture. (Courtesy Dan Rees.)

this time, several divisions were made in selling different portions of the property. At some point, the dormitory was converted into an apartment building, but fell to ruin after several years of neglect in the 1980s. The original buildings are gone now and the site of the main college building stood on the site of the former home of Mr. and Mrs. Jack Truesdale on State Route 43 at the west edge of Harlem Springs.

When William McCoy started the Centreville Academy in October 1858, it was in the Stidger Building, named after builder General Henry A. Stidger in 1841. It was home to his store for years and its third floor contained a ballroom that was known all over this part of the state. Groups such as the Masons, Odd Fellows, Knights of Pythias, and Junior Mechanics of Carrollton instituted their lodges in this building. At one time, Reverend H.S. Lazarr taught a high school in this building. It is now owned and operated by Joe Braley. The Centreville Academy was taught by Professors John MacCormac, Samuel Howey, and William Coleman. William H. McCoy was principal and A.J. Thomas was assistant teacher.

When Centreville changed its name, so did the academy, becoming the Carrollton Academy. For awhile, it was held on the southeast corner of what is now Second Street Southwest and South High Street. After this, it was conducted by Reverend Alex Sweeney and his wife in their residence on Liberty Street (now Third Street Southeast). One of its graduates, Louis Jackson, became the court advisor to the King of Belgium. Several of the Daniel McCook family also

This two-story red brick building was built in 1837 and housed the New Hagerstown Academy, which sent many fine physicians, teachers, and businesspeople into the world. (Velma Griffin Collection.)

attended in preparation for attending Kenyon College and the Military and Naval Schools at West Point and Annapolis. A list of other students is in the Carrollton Centennial Edition of the *Free Press Standard*. This school was forced to close its doors when most of its male students volunteered for the Union Army during the Civil War.

The small community of New Hagerstown was home to the New Hagerstown Academy, founded by Presbyterians and built in 1837. It is believed the land was donated by Barnhart Bower, the first settler to nearby Bowerston. The school was a two-story red brick building topped by a bell tower that operated as a college-preparatory institution until the turn of the century. Academics offered were equivalent to a liberal arts degree. Many eminent physicians, lawyers, educators, and business administrators from Carroll, Harrison, and Tuscarawas Counties received their training there. Probably the most famous graduate was John D. Archibold, who became president of the New Jersey Standard Oil Company. A dormitory stood across the road.

Graduation ceremonies for the academy were a grand ceremony for everyone of the community. People from all around the countryside would attend to hear the speeches, mostly in Latin, given by the students. Students would also conduct debates and perform music. The academy hosted many social activities, such as an oyster supper, ice cream socials, cake walks, and lawn games. The last principal of the academy was Professor John Howard Brown. One of the former minister-teachers of the school was always known to carry an umbrella, rain or shine. Years after the academy had closed, the teacher's former home was being cleaned and a bottle of hair dye was found hidden in the rafters of his basement; hence his reason for carrying the umbrella! The school closed when public schools made this type of academic learning obsolete. A historical marker was placed at the site in 1972. There was also a Young Woman's Seminary here that later became the Episcopal church.

On March 24, 1958 at a meeting of the Carrollton PTA, 47 people met to discuss the opening of a school for students with mental or physical handicaps. The Carroll County Council for Retarded Children was formed. This new council met a month later to establish a school called Carroll Hills. A teacher was hired for $3,500 a year. From 1958 until the fall of 1968, classes for trainable students aged 6 to 21 were held in the Carrollton Junior High School Building. In 1968, the program outgrew the single room it was in, so it leased the abandoned New Harrisburg School building from the Carrollton school system. That fall, the program was in its own building with nine students in the community class for ages six through sixteen, and fourteen in the newly-organized Activity Center for ages 16 and up.

In the community, the Activity Program took the place of workshops, which were a part of the program in larger counties, and gave the students a chance to develop manual skills. The workshop portion moved to its own facility on High Street in Carrollton in 1979. This workshop, called Carroll Hills Industries, trains

This early classroom scene from the Carroll Hills School is from when it was held at the New Harrisburg School building. (Courtesy Tom Shearer.)

those who are old enough how to care for themselves, as well as providing them with jobs and an income. It also gives those with the capability a chance to work in mainstream society. In 1984, the New Harrisburg School building was outgrown and a new facility was built on State Route 9, north of Carrollton. This serves as a school for preschool through young adult. Their preschool program includes all children, developmentally challenged or not.

The Carrollton Early Childhood Center was newly opened for the 2002–2003 school year. It is housed in buildings leased from the St. John's Villa. With their facilities moving into new buildings, Carrollton was able to use the old buildings for preschool through first grade. A need for more classrooms came about when the decision was made to hold kindergarten all day every day, opening the elementary building for the remaining elementary students and giving the Bell-Herron a chance to expand some of its programs. The Carrollton Early Childhood Center houses approximately 230 students.

Before the Carroll Hills School was state funded, members had to raise their own support. This hot dog stand was one of the first fundraisers used. (Courtesy Tom Shearer.)

6. One God, Many Faiths

Many of the settlers had journeyed in search of religious freedom and a place where they could serve God as they chose. For many, their religion was the very breath of life to their souls. Just like the schools, the churches often began as one-room log structures. Before these could be built, settlers often met in each other's homes, or during nice weather, in open fields. The preaching was done by traveling ministers called circuit riders, some of whom held services daily during a four-week rotation. With circuit riding preachers visiting infrequently, settlers often performed their own christenings as many children died shortly after birth. It was also common for a couple who intended to marry to live together with the consent of the community until a minister could perform an official ceremony. The woman was called a consort until the ceremony.

The earliest known church in the area, St. Martin's Lutheran Church, was in Brown Township. In 1800, Reverend John Stauch gathered a community of Lutherans at Telpahak, northwest of Malvern, and they later became the St. Martin congregation. In 1827, a parcel of ground was purchased and a building erected for the Lutherans and the Reformed Church. For more than 50 years, they shared the building by worshipping at different times.

Another church from the 1800s was the Bethlehem Presbyterian Church, located where Colfor Manufacturing is today. The exact founding date is unknown. The land was donated by Simons Jenning, who stipulated that if the property ever ceased to be used for church purposes, it was to be given to the township trustees. Eventually, the congregation outgrew the building and relocated to Malvern proper. The cemetery still remains next to Colfor Manufacturing on State Route 183.

Mentioned in an earlier chapter was the Quaker church in Leesburgh. This area also became home to the Leesburgh Methodist Episcopal Church, which started in 1809. It was built of logs and stood at the north end of the present cemetery. From 1829 to 1865, it was serviced by two circuit riding preachers who served over 30 churches.

Leesburgh was also home to the United Brethren Church, which began after 1812. This small denomination was started by Germans living in Pennsylvania in the late eighteenth century. It relied on farmers who preached in their spare

The only remains of the Quaker Cemetery in Leesville are a few stones that are no longer legible.

time. If a preacher was college educated, the denomination looked on him with suspicion. One of the first United Brethren Pastors to Leesburgh was Reverend James "Old Jim" McGaw. A War of 1812 veteran, McGaw thought the residents of Leesburgh were wicked and did not hide this thought. It is said that when he could not convince the wicked to repent, he would use physical force. The residents were not very happy with McGaw, so one day they were awaiting his arrival with eggs in hand. On this particular occasion, he was accompanied by fellow United Brethren preacher Sewill C. Briggs. Upon nearing Leesburgh, they were warned of the group awaiting them. Briggs convinced McGaw to avoid the conflict and they escaped being egged. The United Brethren Church continued on in Leesburgh until 1968 when the entire denomination joined with the Methodist Episcopals to form the United Methodist Church.

In 1813, the first sermon in Pekin was preached by Reverend Thomas Rigdon, a Baptist minister. The congregation gathered in an unfinished building that would later become a hotel operated by Mrs. F. Barr. Reverend Rigdon was brother to Sidney Rigdon, the Mormon who preceded Brigham Young.

Thought to be the "mother" of Methodist churches in the area was Simmons Ridge Methodist in Loudon Township. Located along County Road 28, the church began in the home of a Dr. Adams. A doctor of physics, Dr. Adams came to the Amsterdam area and began practicing medicine until he converted and began preaching the gospel to a group of nine in his home. Eventually, the class began to outgrow the house. Peter Simmons offered the group 3 acres, which they accepted on April 30, 1822, but the land was not officially deeded to them until May 10, 1825. The following year, a log church was erected on the new tract of land and claimed a membership of over 300. It was considered the mother of other Methodist churches because, as membership grew, other churches were built in the area to accommodate the growth. The first to withdraw was Amsterdam Methodist in 1828, soon followed by Kilgore and Harlem Springs. As a result, Simmons Ridge suffered a severe loss in membership. On November 15, 1851, the trustees met with William F. Bricker and agreed to replace the log church with a new building that still stands on Bear Road. Gravestones in the cemetery date back to the 1700s.

The Lutheran church in Carrollton actually began with the Reformed church. Some accounts say these were one congregation that eventually split; others say they were two from the start and were just sharing a building. Either way, in 1813, a group of believers met with Lutheran pastor Reverend John Stauch of New Lisbon and decided to begin a congregation in Centreville. This group and a group of Reformers built a brick structure on the corner of what is now East Main Street and McCook Avenue. It was called the Jerusalem Church. Just to the west of the building was a small cemetery. In 1817, the Lutheran congregation sent a petition to the conference in New Philadelphia asking for a pastor. Reverend John Reinhart was assigned to the congregation and remained until 1822. A congregational meeting was held on February 19, 1847, with Jacob Stemple presiding and John Cline acting as secretary, at which it was decided to immediately build a new Evangelical Lutheran Church in Carrollton. On

The church in the foreground was built by the Church of Christ and the next one was built by the Lutherans. The Church of Christ building is now home to the Family Worship Center.

March 5, 1847, the Evangelical Lutheran Congregation of Trinity Church was legally organized.

The beginning of the Reformed Church is less clear. It is known that the first preacher, Reverend Herbruck, walked from Canton to Carrollton to preach. In April 1844, Reverend A. Stump became the first regular pastor. He foresaw the building of a new frame church on East Canal Street (now Second Street Southeast). The cornerstone was laid in June 1847 and was dedicated in June 1849. Reverend Stump was so popular that the new church was called "the Stump church," but in 1851, he was replaced by Reverend N.E. Gilds.

The only cemetery in Carrollton proper is thanks to the Lutheran, Reformed, and Presbyterian congregations. Located at the corner of Canal Street (Second Street Southeast) and Park Avenue, Grandview Cemetery began next to the log church used by the Presbyterian congregation. When the Jerusalem church moved its building to Canal Street, the coffins were exhumed from Main Street and taken to Grandview Cemetery, which became the final resting place for Centreville's founder, Peter Bohart. With each war the country fought, many of the county's soldiers came to know this cemetery as their final resting place. Today, it still serves area families.

The first Presbyterian sermon was preached by Reverend James Snodgrass in 1819 at the home of William Croxton. Occasionally, preaching was done at the

The First Presbyterian Church in Carrollton was built in 1893. The church provides a free meal to anyone on the last two Mondays of each month.

Built after the frame church burned of mysterious circumstances, Herrington Bethel Methodist Church on Saviour Road still serves the neighboring communities. (Courtesy Jean Scarlott.)

schoolhouse or in a grove until 1825. On December 31, 1821, a meeting was held with missionary Reverend Joshua Beir where a vote was taken and it was unanimously decided that a church should be built. A log church with no plaster or pews was built in the grove in 1825. The only light was supplied by lard lamps. In 1846, they built a wooden structure on the northeast corner of Lisbon and Second Streets. This building was used until 1893 when the building was sold and moved and a new brick structure built for $10,000. At completion of the building, it was paid in full. The brick church was complete with electricity, a pipe organ, and furnishings throughout.

Orphaned at the age of five when his parents were killed by Native Americans, John Herrington worked hard, fought in the Revolutionary War under George Washington, and then settled in the Augusta area. In 1817, he donated some land and logs to Augusta Township for building a church. In 1825, he offered to give the church stone quarried from his land for a new building. He had already built his home from this stone. The congregation did not want to build until a fateful fire forced them to. It was never confirmed, but stories passed down claim all the hymnals just happened to be in Herrington's house when the church burned. The stone church was then built and called Herrington Bethel Methodist Church. It is also known for having one of the only African-American families, the Grays, in its attendance prior to the Civil War. Even more uncommon, two of their sons served in the Civil War. All seven family members are buried in Herrington Bethel's cemetery.

This Scroggsfield Presbyterian church was dedicated on January 24, 1889, while the congregation has been serving the Scroggsfield area for nearly 200 years. (Velma Griffin Collection.)

As mentioned in a previous chapter, Scroggsfield Presbyterian was begun in an open field and was the reason the village received its name. The first congregation was called Mount Scroggs. The original 20-foot by 30-foot-square log church was enlarged in 1833. Ten years later, it was replaced with a frame structure. In October 1850, this structure burned and was replaced with another frame building. In 1879, this building burned to the ground and yet another frame structure was built, which also burned, in 1887, while the congregation was singing the 77th Psalm. The sexton called out from the gallery, singing ceased, and everyone left calmly. When they saw that the fire was out of control, members went back in and carried out seats, books, the pulpit, and anything else they could. When the building fell in, the service was completed on the lawn. The current building was built by Robert McLaughlin and donated by Robert George, founder of Scroggsfield. It was organized as an Associate Presbyterian church, and in May 1958, it became a member of the United Presbyterian Church of North America. In June 1983, the church became a member of the Presbyterian Church of the United States.

About the same time, the Methodist Episcopals were gathering on the west end of Main Street. The year was 1816 and they called themselves "Wesleyites," or followers of John Wesley. Until a log church was built in 1820, they too gathered in various homes. The itinerant pastor traveled by horse carrying a Bible and a hymn book. The log church was two stories high and stood on 290 West Main Street.

This church building served well until after the formation of Carroll County. The congregation gathered temporarily in the jury room of the old courthouse, while a one-story brick church was built in 1841 on the same site. In 1900, the congregation built another brick church and moved to Second Street Southeast. This church was added on to in 1928 and again in 1968. A parsonage was built next door in 1913 when the church became a single point charge, meaning they no longer used a circuit riding preacher; instead, one preacher presided full time. The church now holds two services every Sunday.

The Zion Lutheran cemetery in Sherrodsville was established before the church when two-year-old Eve Beamer died on September 18, 1816. The members of the congregation gathered in homes for worship until 1821. July 16, 1821 was the first day of construction on the log church. It was replaced by a frame building in 1845. Like so many other churches of the time, this church was consumed by fire on November 8, 1930. By that time, the congregation had already consolidated with Bethesda Lutheran, so as of April 30, 1929, the Zion Lutheran discontinued.

Sometime after 1820, a Friends church was started in Augusta. A member of the Sandy Spring Society of Friends in Hanoverton, Ohio, Stephen McBride received a land grant from President James Monroe in what is now Augusta Township. On December 12, 1818, 1 acre of this land was deeded to the Augusta Meeting House. The Sandy Spring Meeting was held there once a month. On October 12, 1825, another acre adjoining the first on the north side was added. A schoolhouse sat on this second parcel that was built in 1810 and called the Augusta "Friends" School. On June 13, 1840, it was decided to build a log church.

This image shows the Friends Church in Augusta. The only remains are the graves of a cemetery straddling Carroll and Columbiana Counties. (Velma Griffin Collection.)

The labor was donated and work began on June 18, 1840. It was completed in the fall of 1841. This was a silent Quaker meetinghouse and meetings were held in this church for over 30 years. With a growing congregation, a newer and larger brick meetinghouse was built in 1877. By 1900, the congregation was strong and special stalls were constructed to protect their horses from inclement weather. Soon, the members began moving away and others passed away. The roof was in need of major repairs; rather than take a chance, they had the building torn down. The meetinghouse met for the last time in 1946.

The Leavittsville United Methodist Church began in 1825, but did not have an official home until 1830. The very crude building served until a new one could be constructed in 1845. Unfortunately, this building was destroyed when it was struck by lightning in 1902. With insurance money and several volunteers, a new building was constructed and dedicated just six months later. In 1956, the congregation purchased the old Leavittsville School building across the road and now uses it as a Fellowship Hall. The church was added on to in 1986, and for the first time, had indoor plumbing.

The Leavitsville United Methodist Church recently celebrated 175 years of service. (Velma Griffin Collection.)

In Kilgore, the German Reformed church members shared a building with the Lutheran and Presbyterian congregations. The land for this common meetinghouse was purchased in 1827 by the trustees of each denomination. The two-story log building with pulpit and gallery stood near the present Lutheran church. The Presbyterians went out on their own in 1828 and built a brick church. In 1861, separate buildings were constructed for the Lutherans and German Reformeds. Emmanuel Lutheran built a brown frame structure that became a garage when it built a new building in 1887. By 1993, only 15 regular members were left and it was voted by these members to close the church on July 4, 1993.

A Methodist church was started in Augusta in 1827. Begun as prayer meetings in the home of Mrs. Weston, the members later met as a church in the old Wesleyan Church. It was a very small and somewhat dilapidated building and stood where the Leyda and Hague burial lots are in the Mt. Zion Cemetery. It was first a Methodist Episcopal church. The current church was built around 1840 and has been maintained by descendants of the first members. Soon after this church was built, the congregation no longer had circuit riding preachers. Reverend James Rogers came to serve Mt. Zion, which still meets every Sunday.

In the summer of 1831, Alexander Boyd, James Hatley, and Daniel McAllister were meeting in their respective homes for Bible study when they sent a request to the Presbytery of Steubenville to form a Presbyterian church. Reverend C.C. Beatty of Steubenville was sent to fill the appointment. The first services were held in Boyd's barn on what is now Channel Road. A formal request was made in the fall and a church was organized in Mechanicstown. The church was called Corinth United Presbyterian Church. There were 35 members and services continued to be held in various homes until a building was constructed. The cost of the building was $618 and it was used until 1874 when the need arose for a new one. The plan was to build a one-story brick church. When the contractor was delayed until the following year, the congregation decided to build a two-story church with an auditorium on the second floor instead. The church was finally completed in June 1876 with a dedication service on June 11. The service was so large that it filled both floors.

Fifty years after it was organized, the present Stillfork United Presbyterian Church in Augusta Township was built. According to the records in the Hartville Presbytery, David Hyatt appeared in 1882 requesting the building of this church. Before it was built, there were two other church buildings; the first was located on a hill south of Pattersonville and given its name because it was located on the banks of the Still Fork Creek. A request was granted to build this church, and on March 26, 1832, it was organized by Reverend James McKean. On June 15, 1832, Andrew Watson and John Potter were ordained, and on the following day, nine members were received into the church. Before it was organized, Mr. and Mrs. Watson used to walk, sometimes with their baby, 10 miles to Carrollton to attend church. A cemetery still marks where this first church stood. Furnishings for this building were very crude. The seats were slabs of unhewn logs with wooden pegs. The pulpit was elevated and reached by a flight of stairs. The pastor was so small that he had to stand on a box behind the pulpit in order to be seen. Even though it was crude, during the summer, two sermons were preached each Sunday. A brief intermission with a light lunch divided the two services.

With a need for more room, a second building was constructed in 1856 between Pattersonville and Augusta. The site was more centrally located and is also marked by a cemetery. This building was occupied for 26 years before the present building was constructed. This last building is brick with stained-glass windows and is located at the west end of Augusta. It was built on land donated by Thomas Conley and cost $7,000 to build. With donations of labor, it was dedicated, debt free, on Sunday, January 28, 1883. A centennial celebration was held on August 25, 1932.

Most of the churches that have been forced to close their doors have either been sold to another congregation or organization, or unfortunately left in neglect. Not so for the Perrysville Methodist Episcopal Church, organized in 1833 with Reverend E.C. Merriman. In 1939, the Methodist Episcopals joined with the Methodist Protestants to form the Methodist Church. A land deed recorded on July 2, 1847 says the land was deeded by Phillip and Ruth Cahill. It served until it merged with the Perrysville Evangelical United Brethren Church on December 8, 1968 to form the Perrysville United Methodist Church. The building sat empty for four years until it was offered to the Carroll County Historical Society, which accepted it on January 19, 1972. A dedication service was held on June 30, 1974. The building still sits empty most of the year, but during the Algonquin Fall Festival, a special service is held and occasionally a special music service may be attended.

The Amsterdam Presbyterian Church was organized by Reverend Joseph Smith of Carrollton by order of the Presbytery of Steubenville on November 7, 1834. It sits just over the Jefferson County line in Carroll County. There were ten charter members, one of whom was William Knox, a ruling elder. The first building was a brick structure that was destroyed by fire and replaced by a frame structure. Then, in 1910, a new frame building was constructed at a cost of $4,000 and dedicated on February 25, 1911.

This church helped start the first Presbyterian Church of Harlem Springs. Organized on November 18, 1838, the first service was held by Reverend John Knox of Amsterdam and was in the home of Isaac Wiggins. When the group became too large, it moved to the schoolhouse. The organization was completed according to Presbyterian policy on May 10, 1843 with 28 members present. Plans were made to erect a building in 1843 and it was completed in 1847. The church stood on a lot between the present Apollo Road and the first alley off VanJack Street, next to the present IGA store. This church served the congregation until 1880 when a new building was erected on the east side of State Route 43. A dedication service was held on May 20, 1880 and the old building was sold to France and Talbott, furniture dealers. Years later, it was torn down. In the years 1906 and 1907, Harlem Presbyterian shared a pastor with the Carrollton Presbyterian Church. In 1923, Reverend K.J. Stewart asked to hold services in Harlem at 2 p.m. on Sundays, while still holding services in the morning for

The Stillfork Presbyterian Church closed in 1979 and now sits empty in Augusta. (Velma Griffin Collection.)

the Carrollton Church. This was accepted by both congregations and worked until 1924 when Reverend Stewart was replaced by Reverend B.J. Yorke. During his time with the church, remodeling and repairs were made to the building. Reverend Yorke served the church for 17 years. Before his retirement in 1941, electricity was added. In 1964, the church merged with the Methodist church in Harlem Springs, and after a six month trial, the members voted to continue. The First Presbyterian Church of Harlem Springs then closed its doors forever.

The Catholic faith found a home in Carrollton in May 1843 when Mr. and Mrs. Fenton Lawler and family settled in the village. From time to time, missionary priests would visit the family and celebrate Mass in their home. On one occasion, Archbishop Purcell of Columbus conducted services at the Lawler residence. If the family wanted to attend a church service, they had to take the train to Oneida, walk 3 miles to Malvern, and attend the services there. They would then return on the evening train. In 1923, they were finally able to establish a parish in the community of Carrollton. The parish of Our Lady of Mercy included the territory of nine of the fourteen townships in Carroll County. Mr. C.A. Stevens, acting as an agent for the Diocese of Columbus, bought the Robert and Jennie Bothwell farm for the church, an 84-acre farm on the edge of the city limits. Construction of the brick church began in May 1924 when the land was excavated. The cornerstone was laid on July 27, 1924. Father Nickel served as

The groundbreaking ceremony for Our Lady of Mercy Catholic Church was held in Carrollton in 1924. (Courtesy George Rankin.)

the contractor with the pews coming from a Protestant church in Akron and the total cost was $10,500 with a seating capacity of 300. The dedication service was held on November 16, 1924 with Bishop Hartley of Columbus. The Catholic Diocese of Steubenville was established on October 21, 1944 and Carroll County was included. In 1953, the current rectory was constructed, and during the pastorate of Monsignor Edward Gilbert, the debts on the parish were paid and new windows added. In 1982, a social hall and religious education building were constructed. For over 30 years, volunteers from the church have provided meals at the Carroll County Fair, which has served as a wonderful fundraiser for the building fund. Our Lady of Mercy will celebrate its 80th year in 2003.

The year 2003 will also mark a dedication of the new facilities of the North American Union Sisters of Our Lady of Charity General Administration Center. The Sisters of Our Lady of Charity in Carrollton can trace their roots to France. In 1641, St. John Eudes founded the Sisters with the idea of helping women who needed a second chance, including unwed mothers, women released from prison, prostitutes, and young girls whose home lives had poor morals. In 1855, the first American foundation was started in New York when some of the French sisters arrived there. In 1948, the newly formed Diocese of Steubenville followed this idea and opened a children's home. When the home was condemned in 1951, the children's home was moved to Carrollton. In the 1990s, the Sisters of Our Lady of Charity merged with the North American Union of the Sisters of Our Lady of Charity. In February 2001, renovation began on the convent to accommodate the ailing sisters and to provide 21 suites. It also houses novitiates and convent community archives. In July 2003, the general assembly met here and the facilities were officially blessed.

Another church in Harlem Springs now nearly forgotten is the United Brethren Church. According to research done by Jack and Dorothy Truesdale, it was built in 1849 at the site of the present cemetery. The account book of Abel Wiggins states that he began collecting payment for the building in March 1849. The total cost of the building and its furnishings was $125, paid for by donations, and Wiggins himself donated $1 of his own money to close the account in April 1850. The building was dedicated on April 24, 1887 by Reverend W.S. Coder. It was a white wood building with a bell tower and stained-glass windows. In 1888, the trustees of the church sold part of the adjoining ground to Lee Township Trustees to be held in trust for cemetery purposes. They paid $75 for this land. Then, in the late 1920s, the church and the remaining grounds were sold in entirety to the township. For a short time, the building was used for a school and then Jack Zollars bought the building and used the lumber to build a house. The church closed because membership became so small in number it could not operate. The only remaining item is the bell from the bell tower that now hangs in the front yard of the Harsh Memorial United Methodist Church.

On December 8, 1841, 18 members of the Carrollton First Presbyterian Church were released as members to join with seven others in forming a new congregation in New Harrisburg. The organization was put into effect by Reverend James McKean and a meetinghouse was built in 1844 behind the site of the present building. It was a frame structure, lighted with candles, measuring 30 by 40 feet. In 1853, the candles were upgraded to oil lamps, which were purchased for $13.50. By 1870, there were approximately 70 members, and on February 3, 1900, the congregation took steps to build a new church. The members donated all the hauling materials, the foundation lumber, and the stone, so the church only cost $3,000 and was completely debt free at its dedication. The bell was an added expense and the money for it was raised by W.H. Campbell. In 1954, the downstairs was excavated by the men of the church to provide a fellowship hall and kitchen, as well as additional classroom space. Over the years, many other remodeling projects have occurred.

In 1841, members of the Seceder and Associate Reform faith got together and formed the United Presbyterian Church in Carrollton. They were then known as the Associate Reformed Church of Carrollton until 1858, when they merged with the Associate Presbyterian Churches and formed the United Presbyterian Church of North America. The Carrollton Church then became the United Presbyterian Church. The present building was constructed in 1886 and had to be rebuilt in 1937 after being struck by lightning. In 1942, the church began sharing a pastor with Scroggsfield United Presbyterian Church and is known as the Carroll

United Presbyterian Parish. Today, the church is a part of the Presbyterian Church of the United States.

Malvern Methodist Church started in 1842 in a frame building that stood where the present brick church stands. The congregation outgrew its frame building and the cornerstone for the brick church was laid on August 2, 1896. The first service was held on December 17, 1896 by Reverend Matthew Moses. A fellowship hall was later added to the rear of the church.

A Wesleyan Methodist congregation was started in Leesburgh around 1843. John Newell, Jacob Millisack, and James Price Sr. built a frame church on land donated by Isaac Holmes. At the dedication service, there was such a large crowd that an outdoor pulpit had to be constructed for Bishop Edward Gray to give the address. During the Civil War, this church became a regular stop for abolitionist speakers. Once the war ended, the church suffered. Many of its members were older and passing away. The remaining congregation began fighting over issues and a split occurred. The Wesleyan Methodist Church was forced to close its doors. In 1870, the Presbyterian congregation remodeled the building for $1,000 and thrived for quite some time until it too became a victim of members dying or moving away. By the turn of the century, the building was again empty. In 1903, it was dismantled and the lumber used in the construction of a new Presbyterian church in Bowerston.

Another church going strong is the Augusta Christian Church, which first met in an old building known as the Baker Church, located at Glade Run Corners. Later, it held its meetings in a Manfull barn. They were first called Bible Christians and their first church was a stone structure constructed in 1842. The land grant was recorded in 1845, a gift from George and Mary Manfull. The church was called Disciples of Christ. No formal records were kept of this church until December 9, 1887, so much of its history comes from various families in the area. The ministers were circuit riders and the baptismal was in a stream on the Sheckler farm. The bell for the old stone church was donated by the same family. When a new church was built in 1881, stones from the original were used in the foundation. In 1887, the church was incorporated under the formal title, Christian Church of Augusta. The church was remodeled in 1929 with new archway lights and new windows.

Harlem Springs was home to Chestnut Ridge Church. Approximately 2 miles southeast of Scroggsfield, it was built in 1848 by the Presbyterian Society. Dr. John Allmon furnished most of the material for its construction and Samuel Carson helped with the carpentry. The land was later deeded to the Methodist Episcopal Church on March 30, 1866 and operated as a Methodist conference until 1893 when it was dropped from the Harlem Springs charge. Even though there was no preaching, a Sunday school was still held for years. In 1913, Reverend Walter Taylor reorganized the church and it became part of the Bergholz charge. An addition of a basement for educational and social purposes was built in 1957 and the pot-bellied stove was replaced with a furnace. The last addition was made in 1985 with a vestibule, restrooms, and the drilling of a well.

The first Methodist congregation in the Harlem Springs area began just east of Harlem Springs in Millensburgh. Known as the Green Hill Meeting House, it started with meetings led by Reverend E. Hayes from February 4 to February 17, 1848. About 40 or 50 persons confessed conversion. On March 4, a class of 27 members was organized. A few days later, it was decided to build a church. On March 6, 1848, a half-acre of ground was purchased from the Wiggins heirs. The building was 44 feet long, 34 feet wide, and 15 feet high. In 1870, the last sermon was preached in this building by Reverend Richard Cartwright. The congregation moved to Harlem Springs. On March 18, 1882, the congregation decided it could no longer repair the building it was in and voted to build a new church, so a beautiful brick building was constructed. In 1964, this church merged with the Presbyterian church and a still newer building was constructed. The land for this building was donated by Robert Harsh in memory of his parents, William and Emma Harsh, so the church was named Harsh Memorial United Methodist Church. Groundbreaking ceremonies were held in March 1968, 120 years after the Methodist congregation began in the area. The stained-glass windows in the new church were from the former building and from the Presbyterian church.

The original United Presbyterian Church was two doorsteps from this present building on West Canal Street (now Second Street Southwest) and is currently the home of Sarah Cassidy. (Courtesy Dan Rees.)

A bell tower stands in the front yard holding three bells, one from each of the churches that became Harsh Memorial United Methodist. The only remnant of the Green Hill Meeting House is the cemetery sitting back in the woods along State Route 43. The second building is now the Lee Township Community Building.

Another Methodist congregation was officially begun in the Dellroy area in 1849. Whenever the circuit rider came through, church was always in a different location. The circuit rider first began preaching in 1830 in a grove of trees not far from the present church. Then, in 1849, a Methodist Society was organized by Reverend Daniel Mitchell from the Carrollton Charge. A frame church was built and donated by Isaac Russell, and Reverend Sheridan Baker agreed to serve for the sum of $200 a year plus board for himself and his horse. By 1868, the church needed many repairs, and in 1870, Reverend Henry Harrison held a series of "World's Meetings" that lasted for six weeks and claimed 200 converts. But it was 1888 before the church received its much needed repair work. During Reverend Nulton's ministry in the 1890s, a parsonage was built. Then, in 1912, as the sexton was lighting the gas lamps for prayer meeting, an explosion occurred and engulfed the building in flames. The pulpit and a few small items were the only things saved. That very night, Charles Slates, William Snee, William Thorley, and Mel Lytle each pledged $500 toward rebuilding. Thanks to the faithful members who donated their labor and money, the church was rebuilt. Prior to 1965, the Dellroy minister was assigned to four churches: Dellroy, Leavittsville, Baxter's Ridge, and

The Union Valley Church was razed in 1988 when no one offered to purchase the building. (Velma Griffin Collection.)

Union Valley. More recently, it became a two-point charge with just Dellroy and Leavittsville on the circuit.

The same year, a Methodist church was built in Kilgore. When the society was first organized, it met in the home of William Kneen. Then, on January 18, 1849, a half-acre of land was given to the church from William and Catherine Albaugh. The next spring, a frame church was constructed with seating for 300. In 1894, a new church was constructed and the old building moved a short distance away to be used as a town hall. Today, the Kilgore United Methodist Church is on the same circuit as Harsh Memorial in Harlem Springs.

Union Valley Church used to stand just north of Atwood Lake in Rose Township. It is estimated that it began in 1850, but there is little known about its beginnings. In 1927, the building burned after an accident. It was customary to fill the stovepipe with newspaper while cleaning the stove to keep birds out. When the ladies were finished cleaning, they were not able to remove the newspaper. Someone decided to employ the long pole used to light the oil lamps, which caught the newspaper on fire. The paper flew out onto the roof and the building was soon engulfed in flames. By 1939, the church was part of the Dellroy, Leavittsville, and Baxter's Ridge charge. In 1963, it split with Baxter's Ridge to become a two-point charge. By the 1980s, the membership had greatly dwindled and it was decided to close the church.

Methodism appears to have been the denomination of choice for early Carroll County citizens. In 1850, another Methodist Society was formed in New Hagerstown. It was called the Bethel Meeting House and was part of a circuit with Centreville, Pleasant Hill, Green Hill, and Baxter's Ridge. A brick church was built for $830. It was torn down in 1890 and replaced with a frame building. In 1924, this building was destroyed by fire and replaced in 1925. The last known history of this church was that it was part of the circuit with Leesville, Perrysville, Sherrodsville, and New Cumberland.

In 1820, Lewis Harsh moved to the Washington Township area from Washington, Pennsylvania and donated a plot of ground where the Harsh Meeting House was constructed. This building was used for several things: on Sundays, it was the meeting place of the Lutherans, Reformeds, and Presbyterians; during the week, it was a schoolhouse; and when the community needed a place to hold meetings, Harsh Meeting House was the place. Then, in 1845, the German Reformed congregation decided it wanted a building of its own. This time, Lewis Harsh's son Phillip donated the land and the Harsh United Church of Christ was built. For several years, the sermons were still given in German.

It is not clear when people began meeting for services in the Petersburg area since they too gathered in private homes prior to the building of a house of worship. The earliest building was the Morrison Meeting House, built in 1854. The circuit riders who served the church were paid $8 a year and given a horse. Lodging and meals were provided by the wealthier members of the church. This church also served as a meeting hall for the community. Before the Civil War, several members began wearing the butternut emblem showing their support

The Mt. Pleasant United Methodist Church is shown here prior to the 1966 additions. The two front doors were replaced by a single entrance when another addition was made in 1976.

for slavery. A quarrel ensued and membership split. A small group moved a few miles away and built the Pleasant Hill Methodist Church on State Route 332. The land for this building was donated by Henry Brooks in 1854. The members who wished to remain at the Morrison Meeting House formed a Methodist Protestant Congregation in 1856. They remained in the Morrison Meeting House until 1870, when a subscription was taken up to build a new church after a revival meeting. Capper Ready McCort donated additional acreage and a new building was erected. Mt. Pleasant Methodist Protestant Church was built in 1872 at a cost of $3,051.75. The dedication service was conducted by Reverend W.J. Holland and Reverend J.H. Hamilton on December 9, 1872 with a membership of 99; by 1898, membership numbered 182. The church remained on the Dellroy circuit until October 1949 when the Perrysville Charge was formed. When the United Brethren churches and the Methodist churches merged, the name was changed to Mt. Pleasant United Methodist. In May 2000, Mt. Pleasant became a single-point charge. Reverend Wayne Scott had the honor of being the first pastor to this new single point charge. Membership for 2002 was 209 and many descendants of the charter members still attend.

Not too far away in Palermo, another Methodist church was organized in 1856. Its first pastor was William Baldwin. The logs for the church were purchased from the former Mt. Tabor Church by George K. McCaskey. This church was torn down in 1862 and replaced with a frame church, which served the congregation until 1906 when a new frame church was built. Land for this new building was purchased from Sarah E. McCaskey. When membership dwindled, the church members voted to close and the church now stands empty.

In 1858, a Catholic congregation was organized in Malvern. It was called the St. Francis Xavier Church and a brick church was built in 1882. For some reason, it was rebuilt in 1884. This church was under the direction of the Diocese of Columbus, Ohio and had a parochial school with 50 students. Reverend Father A. Dengler was in charge.

Sometime before 1863, Methodist Church South was begun in the southern part of Perry Township. It was located at a place called the "Confederate Cross Roads" because the church was pro-slavery. It was dedicated by Edson B. Olds, who addressed a Vallandingham meeting in a grove north of Carrollton in 1863. It is unfortunate that the exact location and more information on this congregation are not available.

Another church that has nearly been forgotten was the Dellroy United Presbyterian Church. It was created in 1869 by a merger of the Big Springs Church and the Fairmount Presbyterian Church. Big Springs was founded on September 26, 1821 and located on the existing State Route 542 toward Magnolia.

The Palermo United Methodist Church, shown here in 1958, closed in the 1980s. (Velma Griffin Collection.)

The Fairmount Church was at the north end of Atwood Lake and was founded on January 11, 1829. Dellroy United Presbyterian was located off the existing Antigua and Edgewood Roads in Monroe Township.

A Catholic church was established in Sherrodsville in 1883 and was dedicated to St. Francis of Assisi. Reverend H.B. Dues, a pastor from Dover, came to organize the parish. It was officially begun on February 18, 1884. Prior to this, Holy Mass had been said in the house of John Sweeney at Hazelton, a small mining camp nearby, with a sewing machine serving as the altar. Once it was established, Father Dues sent his assistant Reverend Walter Ross, to take care of this parish, and shortly thereafter, he was appointed as pastor of Sherrodsville, Bolivar, and Morges. Father Ross built the first church, which was destroyed in tornado-like winds and later rebuilt. During the pastorate of O.M. Capuchin, 9 acres were purchased for a cemetery. Between 1884 and 1888, Father Lane, then at Morges, had charge of the Dellroy and Sherrodsville Missions. It was during his pastorate that the church in Dellroy was sold.

In 1906, a large tent meeting was held in Carrollton, which resulted in the building of the Tabernacle. Dick Albright, co-director of the Albright China

Now the site of Tinlin's in Dellroy, this Catholic church closed in the late 1880s. (Velma Griffin Collection.)

This picture, taken after 1913, is the Carrollton First United Methodist Church, which is known for its yellow bricks. (Courtesy Dick Griffin.)

Company, and his wife Tillie were instrumental in starting the services. This church was inter-denominational. No records exist showing how many original members there were, but by 1921, there were nearly 450. In 1923, it was incorporated as the Holiness Tabernacle Association. Meetings continued to be held during the summer months until 1938 when a group expressed its interest in starting regular church services. In 1944, services began being held all year long under the pastorate of Reverend Florence B. Dray. During her pastorate, they joined with the Wesleyan Methodist denomination. The building was then partitioned off to provide a sanctuary and parsonage. In the spring of 1979, during the pastorate of Reverend Roy Wade, a building fund was started and lots were purchased on the corner of 12th Street and Darringer Avenue. By October of that year, a new parsonage and sanctuary had been constructed. Today, the original building is used by the One Way Youth Center, a non-denominational, non-profit, church-based center for the teens of Carroll County who needed a place to hang out after school.

The One Way Youth Center began in 1988 through a combined effort of several area churches. A youth pastor named David Nelson began meeting with a small group of youths from the various churches in the parsonage of the Carrollton First United Methodist Church, and by 1989, they were meeting in the basement of Dr. Carl Winters's dentist office on Third Street Northeast. Soon outgrowing this space, the center obtained the former Tabernacle building, and now offers

The Carrollton Baptist Temple celebrated 50 years on June 22, 2003. This is also the home of the Carroll County Christian Academy.

many activities and outings for the areas teens. A board of trustees oversees the needs of the youth center.

The Church of Christ began on the American Frontier in the early 1800s by men like Alexander Campbell and Barton Stone. The denomination in Carrollton was organized in 1913 with Elder J.A. Brown as pastor. They first met in the Opera House, which was located on Second Street Northwest until June 1914 when a church was constructed at 225 North Lisbon. The first building, constructed of brick, cost $12,000 and over one-third of this amount was raised during the first service. A total of 52 people signed their names as charter members in 1914. Over the years, the congregation had formed a strong relationship with Mt. Olivet congregation of Washington Township. In 1931, that church closed its doors and many of its members joined the Carrollton church. In 1987, the church relocated to Moody Avenue. From 1926 to 1938, the church members served meals at the Carroll County Fair to help meet expenses. The tradition is continued today by the Christian Women's Fellowship at the Algonquin Fall Festival. Money earned from the food stand there is used to support special projects.

The Carrollton Baptist Temple was founded in June 1953 through the efforts of Reverend Robert McDonald and a number of interested people. Between 1953 and 1956, the congregation met in a storefront on East Main Street. From the beginning, it has been an independent, fundamental, missionary Baptist church. A portion of the property where the church sits now was purchased in 1956. A 30-foot by 70-foot concrete block building was constructed, and by 1962, the congregation had outgrown that structure. An additional 7 acres were purchased and a 9,000-square-foot church was built. On July 28, 1963, a 325-seat auditorium was dedicated. In 1982, the church wanted to reach more than just its congregation, so the Carroll County Christian Academy was opened, starting with 22 students. Today, the average attendance for kindergarten through high school is 140. As a result of so much growth, the building was again added to in 1991 when an additional 12,000 square feet were added. This new addition holds a gymnasium, four classrooms, a kitchen, locker rooms, and three meeting rooms.

A more recently developed congregation is the Wesley Evangelical Chapel, 1 mile south of Kilgore. After much thought, ten adults and five children decided in the summer of 1977 to search for a church solid in evangelical teaching. On August 23, 1977, Reverend M. Max Morgan of the East Central Conference, superintendent of the Evangelical Church of North America, met with this group to explain the doctrinal position of the denomination. By September 13, it was unanimously voted to organize a new church and the name Wesley Evangelical Chapel was chosen. Philip Fisher became the interim pastor with morning services held in the Rumley Township (Harrison County) Hall and evening services held in the Perry Township Hall. Mid-week services were held in various homes. In July 1979, 8 acres on Germano Road were purchased, and the church and a parsonage were built. By early 1981, they had outgrown their sanctuary and a new one was built. A dedication ceremony was held on February 28, 1982.

There are so many more churches that once served the communities of Carroll County and outlying areas of which this author has no information, such as Glade Run Church, Baxter's Ridge United Methodist Church, the Seventh Day Adventist, the Lighthouse Church in Leesville, Riley Methodist Church near Salineville, the Evangelical Lutheran Church of Augusta, Pleasant Grove Methodist Church, Jehovah's Witnesses near Carrollton, Bethesda Lutheran, Wesley Methodist and Calvary United Methodist Churches in Sherrodsville, Bible Holiness Chapel west of Carrollton, Carrollton Bible Chapel, Dellroy Church of the Nazarene, First Christian Church of Malvern, Malvern Church of Christ, Lutheran Church in Perry Township, Mt. Tabor Methodist Episcopal, Carrollton Church of God, Assembly of God in Carrollton, Vo-Ash Chapel, and North Suburban Church of Christ. With this lengthy list and the histories given, I feel it is safe to say that a strong Christian Faith is held in the Carroll County area, no matter what the denomination is.

7. The Civil War Years

After Fort Sumter was fired upon and several southern states withdrew from the Union, Carroll County's men responded to President Lincoln's call for troops. Parts of companies and regiments for the Union Army were recruited here for the 2nd, 11th, 32nd, 80th, 104th, and 126th Regiments Ohio Volunteer Infantry (OVI). The Civil War called largely on the resources of Carroll County in a variety of ways. The men who readily volunteered and gave their lives to the Union were regarded as heroes.

Attorney Benjamin F. Potts organized a company here for the 32nd OVI on August 29, 1861 and was afterwards appointed its captain. He was born in Fox Township and served with General Fremont in his campaign up the Shenandoah Valley in pursuit of Stonewall Jackson. Following the siege of Harper's Ferry, Captain Potts was appointed colonel of the 126th Ohio Infantry. Later, he organized his 32nd Regiment and was placed in command. The regiment was assigned the 3rd Brigade, which participated in the Vicksburg campaign. There, General Potts was complimented for gallantry in action. He was at the front during the entire siege of Vicksburg and was in command of the skirmish line the day General Grant and Pemberton negotiated the surrender.

In August 1863, General Potts accompanied his men on an expedition into Louisiana. The following year, he was transferred to 2nd Brigade, which launched the Tennessee River expedition. The 17th Army Corps, to which his brigade was a part, joined Shearry in Georgia and participated in the movements at Big Shanty and Kennesaw Mountain. On July 10, 1864, General Potts was placed in command of the 1st Brigade. He took part in battles near Atlanta and official reports of the campaign that closed with the capture of Atlanta. While serving with General Sherman, Potts received his appointment as brigade general of volunteers. After the surrender of the Confederate force, he moved with the army to Washington, D.C. and led his command in the Grand Review. General Potts was discharged from service on January 15, 1866.

Two years later, in May 1868, Potts married Carrollton native Angeline Jackson and returned to the law practice. He became highly involved with politics and became a member of the Ohio State Senate on the Republican ticket. While serving as a member of the state senate, President Grant offered General Potts the governorship of Montana. He refused to accept it at the time. His initial refusal came because the adoption by Ohio of the 15th Amendment to the Constitution depended on his vote. If he had taken the Montana position then, his vote would have been lost by his vacated seat. He accepted the appointment in the summer of 1870. Montana became his final home where he held the office for 12 years. When his term as governor ended, he became a member of the territorial legislature. He died in Helena, Montana on June 7, 1887.

Twenty-two men from the Scroggsfield community saw fit to fight for their country. Among them was Richard B. Donaldson, who was missing in the battle of St. Mary's Church, Virginia. His body was never found and a marker was erected in his honor at the Scroggsfield Cemetery. David Stevenson was killed at the battle of Perrysville, Kentucky and his body returned to Scroggsfield for burial. A.G. Patterson died in a Southern prisoner of war camp. H.K. Allison died in a hospital at Philadelphia, and Robert M. George died at Nashville, Tennessee and is buried in the national cemetery there.

Among the most famous of Carroll County's citizens to participate was the McCook family. They were known as the "Fighting McCooks" because of their participation in the armed services prior to and during the Civil War. Their family home still sits on the southwest corner of Carrollton's Public Square. Daniel

This group of "Civil War" soldiers is from the days of the reenactment at the Algonquin Fall Festival. (Velma Griffin Collection.)

McCook built the brick house shortly after the first courthouse was erected using bricks burned on the same property. Daniel's law office and a store were kept in the corner room and the family occupied the rest of the house until 1853. The four youngest sons and three daughters were born here. One of the daughters, Catherine, also died here. The house became the property of the State of Ohio in 1941. It began operation as a museum by the Carroll County Historical Society in 1981. (It can be visited on the weekends from Memorial Day through Labor Day.) Daniel and nine of his sons served in the Union Army, along with his brother's five sons.

Daniel was actually in Washington, D.C. when the war started, and even though he was 63 years old, he tendered his services to President Lincoln immediately. Serving as a major, Daniel was stationed at Cincinnati and was sent in pursuit of General John H. Morgan when he and his rebels entered Ohio on a rampage. Morgan and his men crossed the Ohio River at Buffington Island. Major McCook led an advance party to oppose and intercept the crossing. In the skirmish that took place, Daniel was wounded and died the next day, July 21, 1863. He is buried at Spring Grove cemetery near Cincinnati.

Of his sons, his oldest, Latimer A., entered the service in 1861 as an assistant surgeon and was soon promoted to surgeon, with the rank of major, of the 31st Regiment Illinois Volunteers, known as "John Logan's regiment". He was

The McCook House built in 1835 by Daniel McCook is now on the National Registry of Historic Places. (Courtesy George Rankin.)

wounded twice and died on August 23, 1869 as a result of wounds and exposure on the field. He is buried with his father in Cincinnati.

The next oldest son was George Wythe, who was one of the first four brigadier generals appointed by the governor of Ohio to command the troops from the state at the outbreak of the war. His military career began when he served as an officer in the 3rd Ohio Volunteer Infantry during the Mexican War. He returned home as its commander. So, when he joined the Civil War, George organized and commanded several Ohio regiments. Having studied law at Ohio University in Athens, after the war George became a law partner of Edwin M. Stanton, who was attorney general of the state in 1871. Stanton also became President Abraham Lincoln's secretary of war. George edited the first volume of "Ohio State Reports." In 1871, he was the Democratic candidate for governor of Ohio, but his health broke down during the canvass and he was forced to abandon the campaign.

The third of Daniel's sons was John James. He served as a midshipman on the frigate *Delaware* in 1842. He died of fever on March 30, 1842 and was buried at Rio de Janeiro. In his untitled autobiography from 1863 to 1870, Admiral David Farragut paid a high tribute to the personal character of Midshipman John McCook.

Robert Latimer, the fourth son, enlisted as soon as the firing on Fort Sumter began and was at once commissioned colonel of the 9th Ohio Regiment among the Germans, enlisting 1,000 men in less than two days. He quickly rose to the rank of brigadier general. In August 1862, while lying ill in an ambulance, he was murdered by Confederate guerrillas near New Market, Alabama.

Son number five was Alexander McDowell, who graduated from West Point in 1852. He served for five years on the western frontier in campaigns against the Native Americans. He was appointed, in April 1861, as colonel of the 1st Ohio Volunteer Infantry, which he commanded at Bull Run. Alexander served throughout the war, and was cited for gallant and meritorious service at Nashville, Shiloh, and Perrysville. By September 1861, he had attained the rank of brigadier general. Soon after that, he was promoted to major general.

Daniel Jr. organized a company at Leavenworth, Kansas and offered his services as early as February 1861. He entered the war as a captain of militia and served successively as chief of staff of the First Division of the Army of the Ohio, colonel of the 52nd Ohio Volunteer Infantry, and commander of a brigade in the Army of the Cumberland. He was chosen by his former law partner, General Sherman, to lead an assault on Kennesaw Mountain. This sixth son was mortally wounded while leading the attack and died on July 17, 1864. His body was taken to Cincinnati and laid to rest with the other members of his family.

Next in line was Edwin Stanton. His first military experience was as midshipman in the Navy from 1854 to 1856. He preferred the Army, recruited a company, and joined the 31st Illinois Volunteer Infantry. His friend John A. Logan was colonel of this regiment, which served at the battles of Fort Henry and Fort Donelson. Edwin succeeded General Logan and followed him in the command of the regiment. He became commander of a regiment, a brigade, and finally a division, serving as a major general under Grant throughout the Vicksburg campaign. In the Chattanooga and Atlanta campaigns, as well as a march to sea, he served under Sherman. He was wounded three times and still returned home. He later became acting governor of the Dakota Territory. While presiding over a public meeting on September 11, 1873, he was shot and killed by a man in the audience who was not in sympathy with the objects of the meeting. Edwin was also buried in Spring Grove Cemetery in Cincinnati.

The next-to-youngest son, Charles Morris, and the youngest brother John James (named for his older brother who died in 1842) both enlisted while studying at Kenyon College. Charles was less than 18 when he enlisted in April 1861. He served with the 2nd Ohio at the first battle of Bull Run. On July 21, 1861, he was passing a field hospital when he saw his father, who had volunteered as a nurse to work among the wounded. Charles stopped to help and the rest of his regiment continued on. When Charles attempted to rejoin his company, he was surrounded by an officer and several troopers of the famous Black Horse Cavalry, who demanded his surrender. His father begged him to do so, but Charles refused and was shot down. Daniel removed his son's remains from the field and later had them sent to Spring Grove Cemetery in Cincinnati.

John James, age 17, joined the 6th Ohio Cavalry in 1862. He was commissioned as lieutenant and assigned to duty on the staff of General Thomas L. Crittenden, commanding a corps of the Army of the Ohio, which became the 21st Corps of the Army of the Cumberland. He served in the campaigns of Perrysville, Stone River, Tullahoma, Chattanooga, and Chickamauga with the Western armies, and in General Grant's campaign with the Army of the Potomac. From the Battle of the Wilderness to the crossing of James River, John J. was commissioned as captain and aide-de-camp of the United States Volunteers in September 1863. He was also brevetted major of volunteers for gallant and meritorious services in action at Shady Grove, Virginia where he was severely wounded. He was made a lieutenant colonel and colonel for gallant and meritorious services. John James left the army with the rank of colonel. He became a prominent lawyer in New York City and a trustee of Princeton University.

Five of Daniel's nephews also served in the military. They were sons of his brother John, a doctor who left his family home in Lisbon, Ohio to start a practice in Steubenville. John's oldest son Edward Moody was appointed major of the 2nd Indiana Cavalry soon after the war began and rose rapidly through the ranks to brevet major general. Unfortunately, he was captured by Confederates behind enemy lines. He resigned from the army to serve as United States minister to Hawaii. He also helped organize and was twice governor of the Colorado Territory (apointed by President Grant), being one of the earliest settlers in the Pike's Peak region. He had gone there to practice law.

The second son was Anson George. He entered the war as a captain and served throughout the entire war in many of the more important engagements in the West and Virginia. He left the service as a brigadier general. According to the

Girl Scouts MaryAnn Tedrick and Karen Eckley show off the restored painting of the Daniel McCook "clan" at the McCook House Museum. (Velma Griffin Collection.)

historical marker, he was a surgeon general who served with distinction in three battles and two campaigns. He became a congressman of New York, serving from 1877 to 1883. From 1883 to 1893, he was secretary of the United States Senate and, from 1895 to 1898, he was chamberlain of the city of New York.

The next son was Henry, who served for a year with the 41st Illinois Volunteer Infantry as a chaplain with the rank of first lieutenant. After the service, he became a Presbyterian minister and won fame through a number of books on theology and natural history, especially his works on ants and spiders. He also served as a home missionary and pastor in St. Louis, Missouri, and then Philadelphia in 1869.

Their brother Roderick Sheldon, the fourth son, was the only one to have other military experience. He graduated from Annapolis in 1859 and served on the west coast of Africa until 1861. He then took active part in aggressive operations at Newberne, Wilmington, Charleston, Fort Fisher, and on James River. He became a commander on September 25, 1873 and accepted the surrender of a Confederate

A parade of Civil War veterans marched through Carrollton in 1910. (Courtesy George Rankin.)

regiment. His last service was in lighthouse duty on the Ohio River. He retired from active service on February 23, 1885 when his health began to decline. He actually died by being thrown from a buggy, which resulted in suffusion of the brain. He is buried with the Daniel McCook family in Cincinnati.

The youngest, also a John James, enlisted early in the war and served the 1st (West) Virginia Volunteer Infantry as a first lieutenant. He went into the Protestant Episcopal ministry and later was a professor of modern languages at Trinity College in Hartford, Connecticut.

Anther man from Carroll County to serve was Thomas L. Patton, who was an officer for the Union. He was also the first child born in Carrollton.

Two companies from the village and township of Augusta served in the Civil War, the 126th Ohio Volunteer Infantry and the 32nd Ohio. The latter became the 26th Ohio Battery. When Thomas Hendricks, the first to be killed, fell at Cheat Mountain from a shot through the forehead, his remains were sent home to be buried near his childhood home.

From Lee Township was native-born James Holder. He studied in the Lee Township School and joined the law firm of Fimple, Holder, and DeFord. In 1862, he enlisted as a soldier in Company D, 80th Ohio Volunteer Infantry. In May 1863, Holder lost his right arm from a cannon shot in Jackson, Mississippi.

He was then captured by Rebels and sent to Atlanta. From there, he was sent to Libby Prison at Richmond, Virginia and then on to Annapolis where he was paroled. When he came home, he attended Harlem Springs College and taught school for two years. In 1866, he was elected probate judge and began practicing law again. Holder died on May 19, 1914.

During the Civil War, a raid was made on a railroad in Georgia by a band of Ohio men from General Mitchell's army. One of the men caught and executed was William Campbell of Fox Township. His mother was Jane Morgan, cousin of Confederate General John H. Morgan. Mrs. Jane Morgan Campbell's sister Keziah Morgan Allison also lived in Fox Township.

The most prominent activity in our area was the engagement of General John H. Morgan and his men with local citizens. On July 25, 1863, General Morgan stopped to have dinner with his cousin Keziah Allison. Allison was not a southern sympathizer, but when she saw the ragged, tired soldiers, she felt sorry for them. While they ate, they discussed their family tree and traced it back to Kentucky. J. Scott Lewis, in an article entitled, "The Relentless Ride of R.M. Crabbs," says that Morgan and his men consumed 14 loaves of bread, 2 pounds of butter, 2 gallons of honey, and 18 gallons of milk. Once fed, Allison gave Morgan a clean shirt and he continued on his way. Several of his men who were wounded stayed with Allison, only to be taken prisoner by the Union Army.

The next morning, Sunday, July 26, 1863, Morgan and his men awoke in the village of Bergholz, several miles south of the Allison farm. Two scouts rushed in to announce they had exchanged shots with Union soldiers. Morgan and his men headed toward Salineville. With them was not only a large amount of boots, shoes, and calicos, but a number of horses they had stolen from the neighborhood. They met with more opposition than they had expected. When they passed through Norristown, a prominent citizen by the name of Shaw had one of his best horses stolen by one of Morgan's scouts. Prior to this time, Shaw had been a southern sympathizer, but the stealing of his horse changed his mind. At Salineville, they were driven back toward Norristown. A number of captives were taken and imprisoned in Augusta. The 15 men wrote their names and other bits of army lore upon the walls of their prison. The building was owned by B.T. Norris and had been a meat market prior to the war. Norris never erased their information, but when the building was later sold, the new owner apparently did not realize the historical significance as the information was then destroyed. The men were taken from Augusta to Columbus as prisoners of war.

From Fox Township, Morgan and the rest of his men headed north for 2 miles before turning east to Beaver. The men had been running from Union General James Shackleford and his men. Shackelford was reinforced by local citizens, who were angered by the stealing of their goods. The citizens turned out to aid, carrying guns, corn cutters, clubs, and any available item that could be used to bludgeon. One young man is said to have returned home afterward to discover his gun was not loaded. When Morgan and his men entered Salineville, Morgan sent scouts ahead. They returned with the report that Union soldiers were already there. Shortly thereafter, they were attacked from the rear by Major W.B. Way and his 9th Michigan Cavalry. All but 250 of Morgan's men escaped. Two of the men were killed and are buried in West Grove Cemetery near Monroeville.

Morgan and his men who escaped headed west and were passing near Riley's U.M. Church on State Route 39 when they were fired upon by the East Township Home Guard. Many of Morgan's men were wounded in the skirmish, and the people of Fox Township took them in and tended to them until the Union troops came for them a few hours later. Morgan once again escaped and continued north into Columbiana County. Then he turned to the southeast and was most likely planning to cross the Ohio River into West Virginia. This time, he encountered Captain James Burbick. Instead of fighting, the two sides talked. Morgan agreed not to kill or injure anyone else and not to destroy any more property. With this agreement, the Union promised to allow him to leave the state unmolested. Morgan did not get very far when his command met with Major George Rue and the 9th Kentucky Cavalry. When Major Rue demanded his surrender, Morgan said he had already surrendered to Captain Burbick. Rue refused to accept that surrender and demanded he surrender to him. Morgan had no choice. This ended a 3-state, 17-day raid that had begun in Kentucky, gone into Indiana, and then across Ohio. The only thing accomplished by Morgan's raid was tens of thousands of dollars of property damage throughout Indiana and Ohio. Morgan's first night in prison was at a hotel in Wellsville; from there, he was sent to the Ohio Penitentiary in Columbus. After only four months, Morgan escaped and rejoined the Confederate Army in Kentucky. This was the northernmost engagement between sizable military forces of the Civil War.

When the news of Morgan's Raid reached Carrollton, the courthouse bell sounded the alarm. The residents quickly began hiding their valuables. Mrs. Makin of Leesville brought a valuable horse into the house. Others buried jewelry and money in their gardens or threw them down wells, some of it to never be recovered. Many of the boys who were serving with the Union were home on furloughs and quickly joined in the fight. While the men prepared to go to battle, the woman prepared food. At noon, a lunch was offered on the parade ground. In the afternoon, the courthouse was made headquarters and the ladies prepared supper, spreading a table on the public square, which they loaded with plenty of food.

Although the Civil War occurred to preserve the Union, President Lincoln's Emancipation Proclamation abolished slavery as well. Before it was effected, slaves were not free. It is not surprising that Morgan and his men were not welcomed in this part of the country. Many of Carroll County's citizens were abolitionists and were highly involved with the Underground Railroad. Very secretive routes led slaves from the southern states to freedom in Canada. This escape route is said to have been organized by Levi Coffin, a wealthy Quaker of North Carolina, who conducted his campaign in and around Cincinnati. The name came from the fact that African-American slaves from the South crossed the state without ever being seen. Ohio was considered a free state, but the Fugitive Slave Bill of 1850 made it unlawful to help escaped slaves; thus, they were not safe anywhere in the United States. This bill gave slave owners the right to organize a posse anywhere in the United States to recapture a runaway and courts, police, and private citizens were obliged to help them. If they did not oblige or were caught helping the escaping slaves, they could be fined, imprisoned, beaten, or even killed. Free citizens put their own lives in danger to help the slaves gain freedom. Around 50,000 slaves were assisted by the Underground Railroad in making their escape prior to the Civil War. The "operators" of the "stations" not only provided food for their guests while they were with them, they also saw that they were furnished with everything necessary to get them to the next station.

Leesville was probably the most active village in helping slaves. The anti-slavery movement started in this area in the early 1840s. The Wesleyan Church became a regular stop for abolitionist speakers including Frederick Douglas, William Lloyd Garrison, Wendell Phillips, Abbe Kelley Foster, Parker Pillsbury, and Lucretia Mott.

John Millisack was a merchant whose store was located on the northwest corner of the square in Leesville. His home was just east of town and slaves were led there from Port Washington in Tuscarawas County and Mount Pleasant in Jefferson County by himself and Joseph Burr. The Millisacks would hide the

Dedicated on May 25, 1969, this marker commemorates Morgan's raid through Fox Township.

slaves in an attic under the sloping roofs on either side of their two second-story bedrooms. The attic was reached by way of a trapdoor in the ceiling of the back porch and a ladder that was pulled into the opening. From Leesville, they would travel to Perrysville and then to Salem, Columbiana County via Baxter's Ridge or Scroggsfield. This trip was frequently made by concealing the slaves under loads of hay or in wagons with false bottoms. Others traveled at night.

Another stop on the Underground Railroad in Leesville was the home of John R. Deal. He owned a mill at Leesville and slaves were hidden there until it was safe to continue. Others in the Leesville area who helped with this Underground Railroad were Horatio and Richard Roby, Samuel Holmes, and Dr. Joseph S. Burr.

The next known stop from Leesville was in Perry Township at Mordecai Amos's home, built in 1841 with the purpose of building a secret room in mind. The room was reached by a trapdoor in the floor of the pantry and camouflaged by a "set in" porch. The brick wall in the basement was solid with the exception of one brick, which was removable for communication.

The next stop was probably the home of Fred Campbell in Kilgore. Here, slaves were hidden in the attic of the brick home, which was accessed by a trapdoor from the second-floor hall into the attic.

Carrollton was heavily divided on its feelings toward slavery, and even though two homes razed in the 1960s and 1970s were said to have been built as stations, it is doubtful they were ever used. One of those was the McCoy house on West

This image shows the Circle at Leesville, including the Township Hall, which hosted abolitionist speakers during the Civil War.

Main Street. It would have been too great a risk to pass anyone through here.

Augusta Township is said to have had at least one station. It was near Stillfork Valley and was known by code number, as the owners were rarely mentioned by their real names.

About 1837, the pastor of the Scroggsfield church was replaced by Reverend John Patterson. Besides preaching on Sundays, Patterson ran a gristmill six days a week and conducted a select school in the second story of his spring house. He strongly opposed slavery and preached many anti-slavery sermons. His home and the home of Scroggsfield founder Robert George became stops on the Underground Railroad. George's home had a false basement where slaves could be hidden. A section of the basement had a false wall that divided the area. The door to this secret room was through a cupboard door set high in the wall. Of course, there really was no cupboard. The George family used to tell of a family that was once hidden in their basement. The family had a boy about six years old who was allowed to come out and play with the other kids in the evening. During the day, he had to stay in the secret basement.

Another house on the Underground Railroad was in Pattersonville. It was a small room built under a porch. The house was made of brick and the secret room was reached just like the one in Scroggsfield.

Secrecy was very important because even though there were many abolitionist supporters, there were just as many who supported the South called "Copperheads." Some thought the name came from the idea that they would ambush and strike like the snake. It actually came about because supporters would wear copper buttons to distinguish themselves. A secret society known as "The Knights of the Golden Circle" was made up of members who bitterly opposed the Abolition movement. It was active as far back as 1834, but the name was not official until 1855. The group was discovered by Lieutenant Thomas L. Patton, who was appointed and commissioned as a recruiting officer for the county. They would hold meetings in abandoned houses or graveyards. Two known places were the Champer Cemetery in Center Township and the Green Hill Cemetery in Lee Township. Pamphlets were distributed to discourage the enlistment of soldiers in the Union Army and were considered very disloyal. Following the Battle of Chickamauga, soldiers of the 11th Regiment Ohio Volunteers saw the names of three Knights of the Golden Circle from Carroll County printed on grain sacks captured from Rebels on September 9, 1863.

Another local participant of the Civil War had no part in the fighting. Her name was Mrs. Mary E. Kail, known for her poems "Crown Our Heroes" and "Ohio." Most of her poems were patriotic in theme and appeared in many newspapers. These poems were often recited or sung on numerous public occasions. In 1864, she and her husband Gabriel S. Kail purchased a 107-acre farm from Jacob Millisack. Financially, the Kails did not do well and Gabriel mortgaged the farm three times before selling in 1877. Mary did her part to earn money through her poetry. Among her writings were campaign songs for the Republican Party. Those songs helped her gain a job as an auditor in the Treasury Department at

Washington, D.C. in the early 1880s. When Democrat Grover Cleveland won the 1884 election, Kail lost her job. She appealed to the secretary of the treasury, Daniel Manning, for help. When the appeal did not work, she turned back to her writing. Shortly thereafter, her book *Crown Our Heroes and Other Poems* was published. The Kails returned to Leesville, and in 1888, Gabriel died. When the Republicans were voted back in that same year, Mary regained her job and moved back to Washington where she died on January 28, 1890. Copies of her poems "Crown Our Heroes" and "Ohio" can still be found in Henry Howe's *Historical Collections of Ohio.*

After the Civil War, a post office was established in Washington Township. It was started on February 20, 1868 and was named in honor of General Ephraim R. Eckley, who was a member of congress from that district at the time. Mail was delivered three times a week. Service was discontinued on January 17, 1891 and delivered to the area from Specht. For years, the area was called Figley's Mill, and as far back as 1844, was owned by Andrew Boyd.

Long after the war, reunions were held throughout the county. Men from New Hagerstown gathered in Bowerston on August 24, 1882 with others who had served in the 126th Ohio Volunteer Infantry. The town was decorated with flags, evergreens, and banners saying, "Welcome 126th O.V.I., Welcome," "God Bless Our Boys," and "Welcome, Brave Boys." By noon, 2,000 people had gathered. The New Hagerstown and Leavittsville Bands played as men arrived. Captain Wallace's Company from New Hagerstown and Captain Rogers's Company from Bowerston all marched to the train depot armed with miniature guns and headed by the Leavittsville Band to meet those arriving from the East.

At the close of the Civil War, a special feature of "internal revenue" drove still houses out of the entire county. An assessor of the Internal Revenue was making a survey of Carroll County and found an illegal still on Sell's farm in Navengall Hollow (an area of Perry Township), which he immediately reported. This particular still was known as "Hoopengarner's whiskey" and the whereabouts of its illicit distilling was probably discovered by the frequent observance of farmers in the immediate area going away from this place with a grain sack thrown over the back of a horse or donkey with a "brown jug" in one end and an equal sized stone in the other.

Prohibition would not take place for another 55 years, but the residents of Carroll County were against liquor as early as 1840. On January 19, 1838, a group of concerned citizens gathered at candle lighting time in a Malvern residence to discuss temperance. The home was that of William Hardesty and the meeting was brought to order by Dr. N. Steel. He served as president of the group with George Hardesty as secretary. It was decided that "all intoxicating liquors" were not to be used as a beverage nor to be trafficked in any manner except in cases of extreme sickness. This feeling carried to other parts of Carroll County and once the Temperance movement began, there was no turning back. Only one person ever tried to open a saloon in Perry Township and he ended up in jail for three months. The Honorable William Adair, who served as a member of the

Constitutional Convention, practiced law in Leesville and was the author of the liquor law.

Those who were bootlegging had to find a way to hide the evidence of creating their own "home brews." One way of doing this was feeding the scraps to the pigs. A small area to the east of Carrollton, near the intersection of Chase and Pageant Roads, became known as Pigtown since this method of disposal was very popular there. Although the name has diminished with the passing of time, there are still many citizens who still refer to the area as Pigtown.

John Millisack's home, also known as the Underground Railroad Plantation. In the photo are later owners Edwin and Doris Preston. (Velma Griffin Collection.)

8. The Turn of the Century

At the close of the Civil War, the citizens of Carroll County remained inactive along the lines of improvement for nearly ten years. The building of the Union School, the construction of public cisterns, the lighting of the streets with oil lamps, and opening a park upon the public square in Carrollton were about all the public improvements until 1872 when the Carrollton Building and Loan Association was formed. This association enabled its members to build new dwellings, improve the older ones, and liquidate certain indebtedness, which opened the door to many new improvements. The first was the erection of a new courthouse, followed by the securing of brick-making plants.

The town council authorized an election held on May 27, 1890 for the purpose of determining whether there should be $10,000 worth of village bonds issued as a bonus to encourage the building of a tile and brickworks, within 1 mile of the public square. Out of the 210 votes, 199 were in favor of the bonds and 11 voted "No." The brickworks were built 2 miles south of town and gave Carrollton a new life. The streets were paved, a new depot was secured, and many private residences went up about town.

Paved roads, telephones, and railroad travel soon brought the need for electricity. The Carrollton Electrical Company was organized in 1894 through a partnership of Judge U.C. DeFord, Junius C. Ferrall, and Virgil Stockon. The plant was put into operation on September 1, 1895 and a contract was entered to light the streets of Carrollton for ten years. At the time, the enterprise was regarded by many as being a foolhardy one and numerous predictions of failure were made. These same people felt the town was not large enough to sustain such a facility. In 1896, DeFord and Ferrall bought Stockon out, continuing to operate the plant until September 1, 1905 when the company was incorporated under the laws of Ohio with a capital stock of $20,000. Despite what the early naysayers thought, the plant had to be increased several times to keep up with the demand of the consumers. Taylor Woodward wrote the following in his history of Augusta:

> Of all improvements and inventions, electricity has benefited the rural people the most. Many 32 volt home light plants were in use in the early

The Carroll Electric Coop building serves the rural areas of Carroll County. (Velma Griffin Collection.)

> 1920s and a few with 110 volt current, but not until R.E.A. (Carroll Electric Coop.) took over, did many of them get electricity.

Charges were determined by the number of lightbulbs used.

A year after the village of Carrollton received electricity, the people voted 183 to 14 to install a village waterworks. A standpipe was erected on the north edge of Carrollton. Now called a water tower, it is located on Garfield Avenue and the original pumping station remains on the edge of town where Park Avenue becomes Andora Road. It was put into operation in mid-April 1896. The water is secured from wells, all more than 100 feet deep, located at the creek bottom northeast of town. There were originally five wells, but with the growth of the village it became necessary to increase the supply. Six new wells were drilled by 1915 and three of the original were abandoned as they were too close together. During the first year of use, there were 80 taps made into the water source and a daily consumption of 15,000 to 20,000 gallons.

Natural gas was introduced in 1906, and according to an old newspaper article, "with electricity for power and light, water to eliminate contaminated wells, gas for cooking and heating, and paved streets to get the town out of the mud, Carrollton was on its way." With all of these additions it is no wonder Carrollton was suddenly a hub of industry in the early 1900s.

One of the earliest industries for Carroll County was coal mining. Throughout the towns and countryside, mines provided an income. Some landowners had private mines called "drift mines" or "country banks," shallow veins of coal that

This image shows one of the mines in Sherrodsville. Coal mining faded and mines like this were closed when state regulations restricted coal use. (Courtesy Dan Rees.)

the landowners could dig with a shovel or pick and haul away in a wheelbarrow. There were half a dozen of these mines in the Conotton Valley in the late 1800s.

The deeper mines were called "drilling," or auger-type mines. A few mines around the Sherrodsville area were called "slope" mines, which referred to the degree of slope, or angle, for entering the mine. There were also several deep "shaft" mines in the Sherrodsville area. One was near the old Sherrodsville cemetery and it produced the most coal in that township. This mine was supposedly large enough to walk from Sherrodsville to a farm outside of town through its shafts.

Because of the mines, small temporary settlements sprung up in the countryside. Stringtown was one of these and was located north of Leesville Lake. A group of miners who hauled coal for the Preston country mine (near present-day Firebird Camp) settled there. Other mining settlements were Fuller, LaJoie, and Phillipsburg. Nothing remains to even tell us where these settlements were.

In the 1900s, a coal pipeline existed from Cadiz through the northeast corner of Carroll County. There was a "Y" east of Carrollton where a pumping station was located. This line consisted of coal that was finely ground and then pumped through with water. When the railroads came through, this method was abandoned as the railroads gave a good price to haul coal in its natural state.

Oil production in the Conotton Valley was big in the 1970s and 1980s. Oil companies established retail stations at Sherrodsville.

Another major discovery and new industry for Carroll County was clay. In 1886, clay was discovered in Malvern by John Kratz and he opened the first clay plant. The business became extremely popular and Malvern had five clay plants running full force at one time: P&M, the Big Four, Deckman-Duty, Robinson Clay Products, and Malvern Clay Company. The Deckman-Duty Company was on the Wheeling and Lake Erie Railroad line and produced high-grade paving brick or blocks. The blocks weighed 7 pounds and the company bragged of an annual production of 8.5 million of these blocks. Many roads throughout Ohio, Michigan, Pennsylvania, and western New York were paved with these blocks.

Around the same time that people were digging the hills of Carroll County for coal, oil, and clay, the California Gold Rush was beginning. Throughout 1898, newspapers all over eastern Ohio were bursting with tales of the fabulous gold finds in California and northern Canada's Klondike. Taking advantage of this great fortune, saloon keeper A.L. Wartman announced he too had discovered gold—in Malvern. Hundreds of people flocked to Shanty Hill farm where the gold was reportedly found. The land all around the cave was greatly sought after and purchased for high dollars. Wartman spent $3,000 on machinery to mine the gold, including a smelter with a 30-ton a day capacity. He also hired a man named John Williams, a native of England who had spent 30 years in the Australian gold fields, to run the mine. A silent partner put up the money for the mining equipment. When asked about the mine, Wartman was indifferent and would not answer questions pertaining to the find.

In November of that year, Wartman was indicted by a Carroll County grand jury on 15 counts of violating state liquor laws. He was convicted when he refused to plead guilty like the other saloonkeepers who were also indicted. Wartman was sent to a workhouse, and upon his release, he did all he could to keep the Malvern gold strike going. He wrote a letter to the *Iron Valley Reporter* the next summer and this time he was eager to give details about the operation. He claimed he needed 12 miners to operate the mine. In 1899, Wartman formed the Ohio Developing Stock Company, along with men from Chicago, Denver, and Seattle. Once the subscriptions were all sold, the investors disappeared. That fall, Wartman was bought out by two Carroll County men expecting to make a small fortune. It was then discovered that the "gold" was merely gold dust loaded into a shotgun and then fired into the rocks. What Wartman had intended to gain by the whole ordeal will never be known, but instead of making a fortune, he too wound up with nothing.

Prior to the Civil War, a law had been enacted by the State of Ohio for each of its counties to provide for their poor. With this law was the establishment of "poorhouses," homes where those who could not provide for themselves, for whatever reason, could live and be cared for while working however they were able. Before this, the paupers were "farmed out," which means they worked for the lowest bidder who entered into a written contract to keep them for one year, for a stipulated amount therein named, which depended on the ability of the pauper to work. Once the law passed, places to house these paupers had to be built and someone was employed to supervise their care and treatment. These homes were tax-supported and were required if a person could not support themselves. It was an alternative to what we would now call welfare. People could request the help, or if the need was likely to be long-term, they were sent to the poorhouse instead of being given relief while they lived on their own. Sometimes people were sent to the poorhouse even if they had not requested help; usually, this was done when they were found guilty of begging in public. But the poorhouse was not a debtor's prison.

The poorhouses were built with a lot of optimism and many believed that this type of housing would provide the opportunity to reform and cure the people in the institutions of their bad habits and character defects that were assumed to be the cause of their poverty. By mid-century, people were starting to question their success. They were actually more expensive than anticipated and did not reduce the numbers of poor people. When the Civil War started, the system was sheltered from the impact of the poverty produced by the war itself. The war created widows and orphans, and it deprived the elderly members of families of the support they might have had in their old age, had their sons and grandsons lived or remained able to work. Oddly, only a small portion of these casualties ever wound up living in the poorhouse, particularly due to special laws that required any needed assistance be provided as outdoor relief to veterans and their families. This relief was given to those outside of the poorhouse that needed temporary aid and the Civil War Pension Plan was instigated. By 1875, poorhouses became the responsibility of the State Board of Charities. Laws were passed that prohibited children from living in poorhouses, and removed mentally ill patients and others with special needs to more appropriate facilities.

When social welfare legislation began, providing for people who would have previously been placed in the poorhouses, the buildings were mainly converted into nursing homes for dependent elderly people. The poorhouses left orphanages, general hospitals, and mental hospitals as their heritage.

The first poorhouse in Carroll County, a 128-acre farm in Union Township, was purchased on May 1, 1839 from Christian Stern. The county paid $2,570 for this farm. On September 9, 1839, a board of directors was appointed by the county commissioners, consisting of William Coleman, Jonathan Kelly, and John McCormack. Edward McCoy was the first superintendent. The land deed was recorded for the poorhouse on August 1, 1842.

On July 6, 1867, a new farm of 286 acres was purchased for $13,600 from George Ebersole and was later expanded to 365 acres. The land from the first poorhouse was sold in 1871 to A. Bothwell and the poorhouse, which was then called the "County Home," was moved to Washington Township. It no longer operated under a board of directors; instead, it was under the management of the county commissioners.

The residents used to grow their own vegetables on the farm with plenty of eggs and milk. They worked from 5 a.m. to 7 p.m. and then in later years, volunteers did the work. (A wonderful account of life at the home in the 1920s is given by Jane Wingerter in her story "Full Circle" in the book *A Carroll County Collage*.) Now 300 acres of the farm are leased out to neighboring farmers and all the needs of the residents are supplied by hired help. Three tracts were set aside for the county dog pound, a cemetery, and a garden. The last time the residents worked in the garden was 1967.

A wing known as the Carroll County Hospital was built in 1937 with county funds and opened for use on April 1, 1938. By the early 1950s, it was difficult to keep the building in decent repair and a bond issue enabled the county to provide the funds to renovate and add a new building. The new building was completed in 1954. Today, the home provides assisted living for persons not requiring complete nursing care. The name was changed to the Carroll Golden Age Retreat in 1988 and is still financed through fees paid by residents and an operating levy. If a resident is unable to pay all or part of the fee, they are not excluded.

Since the first poorhouse, many other organizations and businesses have come into existence with the purpose of helping the less fortunate in mind, including a Department of Health and Human Services and a tri-county improvement committee known as HARCATUS, which includes Harrison, Carroll, and Tuscarawas Counties. There are also service, federated, fraternal, and social clubs, too numerous to name, which are greatly involved in their respective communities.

For residents who do need a more healthcare-orientated facility, there is the Carroll Health Care Center on Longhorn Street. It was built in 1980 and offered 101 beds, one of which is an isolated room. Additions have been made with the most recent being in 2000; it is an Alzheimer wing with 17 beds. Since 1980, a full therapy department was also added. Carroll Health Care Center is a skilled nursing facility.

The Carroll County Home was the second "poorhouse" built in the county and is now called the Golden Age Retreat Center.

Although it was necessary for the county to open a home for its poor, there were many residents who were able to rise above circumstances like the Civil War and the Depression and do quite well. One such person was John D. Archbold. Born on July 26, 1848 in Leesville, John's family moved to Carrollton soon after his birth. His father ran a dry goods store and served as itinerant minister to the Methodist church. According to their neighbors, the family income was meager and uncertain, so these neighbors did what they could to provide the family with vegetables, fruit, and an occasional side of pork. At the age of 14, John left school in Carrollton and went to Salem where he clerked in a general store. By 1864, he had moved to Pennsylvania where he took a job as a driver for a firm of crude oil dealers. By 1870, he was a partner in an oil firm known as Porter, Moreland & Company, who sent him to New York as a representative for the sale of the products of his firm and those of several other companies. In 1875, Porter, Moreland & Company and others in the Pennsylvania oil region became identified with the Standard Oil Company. John went along with the new firm, and in 1879, became a director of the Standard Oil Company of Ohio. Two years later, he was elected to the first board of trustees of the Standard Oil Trust and was one of the liquidating trustees at the time of the dissolution of the

John McTammany is the inventor of the player piano. (Velma Griffin Collection.)

trust. In the years that followed, John served as president of the Atlas Refining Company, the Acme Oil Company, the Solar Refining Company, and the South Penn Oil Company, and was an officer or director for 21 other companies that were formerly component parts of the Standard Oil organization. When John D. Rockefeller retired as president of the Standard Oil Company, John Archbold was elected to succeed him. He served in that position until his death in 1916.

Another ingenious man was Charles Dunster. A self-taught man, he earned his keep working in a blacksmith shop in Leesville. Using the tools of his trade, Dunster created an astronomical clock, which simultaneously kept the time of several large cities around the world. An example of his work is on display at the Stark County Historical Society Museum at McKinley Monument Park in Canton, Ohio. It hung for several years in the chapel at Mount Union College.

Another man for whom many were grateful was John McTammany. As a youth, he served in the Civil War in Nashville, Tennessee. While recovering on a cot, an idea came to him. McTammany returned to Carrollton where he began manufacturing an automated piano, which we now know as the Player Piano. He also invented the organette and perforated music. Some would argue that he stole the idea, but it was agreed in court that John McTammany was indeed the inventor. He may have to share credit with several others throughout the United States and Europe, but in 1881, a patent was issued to McTammany for his invention. He knew how to engineer the piano, but lacked the marketing savvy or financial resources to turn it into a success; thus, the first to be marketed in the United States was the "Angelus," made in 1897 by Edward H. Leveaus, whose patent was for "an apparatus for storing and transmitting motive power." In 1913, McTammany published a book on the history of the Player Piano in which he covered every phase and angle, showing that he was indeed the inventor of the instrument. The piano lost popularity during the Depression, especially once motion pictures were created. McTammany was also the inventor of the original voting machine devised for mass electorates. His machine was a complicated mechanism adaptable to an American political system with a long ballot and electoral rules that changed from one locality to another, thus avoiding the incidental risk of irregular and fraudulent voting.

One of the more lasting items introduced to Carroll County's citizens was that of ice cream in 1890. Robert Patterson was the first person to make ice cream, which he sold in his restaurant and to wholesale trade. His store was located at the corner of Main and High Streets until 1910 when he was elected county treasurer. John Westfall then continued the business in the same location.

Today, we worry about safety releases on automobile trunks, but after 174 children and 2 teachers were killed when Collinwood School in Cleveland burned, Charles Hoffman designed a safety lock for buildings. Called the Hoffman Safety Lock, it was "so simple a child could operate it." The device was noticed by Safety First experts all over the country and contained no springs, never needed to be oiled, and was always ready for use. It was installed on the inside of the door and, with the slightest pressure on either the upper or lower panels of the door, it would open. Hoffman also operated the Star Theater in the old Free Press Standard building. He died of the flu in 1918.

Prosperity for the county is often paralleled with that of the Carrollton Pottery Company. In January 1903, a group of promoters visited Carrollton and worked out a plan to organize the Carrollton Pottery Company. Building operations were begun, and the following August, the first wares were produced. The company started with five ware kilns and four decorating kilns. Eventually, it increased to nine ware kilns and eight decorating kilns, which increased production to more than three times that of the original. All the raw materials (the clay) for this plant were shipped in from Kentucky, Tennessee, and England. As many as 350 people were employed at Carrollton Pottery. In June 1914, half of the plant was destroyed by fire, but was quickly rebuilt and enlarged. The plant was then fireproofed and a sprinkler system was installed. In 1928, the company merged with American Chinaware Corporation, which had offices in Cleveland. Operations continued until 1934 when the plant became defunct. The first cup to come out of the kiln was given to the Carroll County Historical Society by Charles E. Helfrich and is on display at the McCook House Museum.

The same year the Carrollton Pottery Company burned, A.E. and M.F. Albright retired from the Carrollton Pottery Company and several citizens' meetings were called in the interest of starting another pottery facility. On July 28, a meeting was held just before the Chautauqua opened, with a crowd of 300 led by a band, and $32,400 was subscribed. Twenty-four hours later, the original $50,000 bond issue was over-subscribed. The Albright brothers agreed to operate the new china company and ground was broken on October 15, 1914. The first ware was made on March 1, 1915, and by April 5, the first decorating kiln was fired. The new company was called the Albright China Company. It closed sometime in the 1930s.

During their years of operation, both pottery facilities were supplied with wooden boxes from the Newell Box Factory. It was started by Leavittsville resident E.B. Newell around 1908, and purchased by Charles B. Newell and Charles Moreland in February 1911. Moreland sold his interest to Charles Newell in April 1915, making Charles Newell the sole owner. Newell also operated a sawmill that employed 12 to 15 men. Along with supplying all the boxes to the two Carrollton potteries, the Newell Box Factory also handled railroad ties, car lumber, mine props, and hardwood lumber for finishing purposes. This company made 400 boxes daily.

The early 1900s saw many new industries enter the county, such as the Tuscan Tire and Rubber Company, which made rubber products of various kinds. It was incorporated in August 1909 and April 1910 for $120,000. On December 1912, the capital was increased to $500,000 as production of automobile tires began in the spring of 1911. This factory was one of the largest mail order rubber houses in the world. They made Buckskin and Tuscan tires, and were also large manufacturers of druggists' rubber goods, such as gloves. The plant produced its own electricity for power and lighting. By 1915, the daily capacity of tires

The Carrollton Pottery Company was located near High and Fifth Streets. (Courtesy Dan Rees.)

was 300. In later years, another Carrollton company manufactured latex gloves for hospitals.

Before the manufacturing of latex gloves, the building housing this latex company was the skating rink called the Knickerbocker Skating Rink; if not for Ben Specht, it would be completely forgotten. Today, the name Ben Specht would not mean much to sports fans, but in 1916, when he came to visit his sister, Mrs. L. Jones, it made heads spin. Ben Specht placed third in the world's championship roller-skating races held in Pittsburgh in 1915. At the time of his visit to Carrollton, he also held the state record of Pennsylvania and the unpaced record for the mile at 3 minutes, 2 seconds. He also topped the marathon field by skating 26 miles, 385 yards in one hour, 25 minutes, and 15 seconds. Naturally, he had the nickname "Speedy." It is no wonder folks here wanted a race held when they heard of his arrival. It was a 5-mile relay race of Speedy against five of the county's fastest skaters. The racers were Sammy McBee, Whitey McMullen, Frank Barr, Hi Berlin, and Brown Davis. The race was held at the Knickerbocker Skating Rink. One mile would equal 22 circuits of the rink. Admission for the event was 25¢. Speedy easily outraced the five men and is said to have skated another 11 laps before realizing the race was over. It is also said that he skated at a rate of 17 miles per hour.

When the rink closed, it was rented by Affiliated Hospital Products, which manufactured disposable hypodermic needles, catheters, Penrose drainage tubes, wheelchair seat covers, and prosthetic knee sleeves. The company at first leased the old skating rink in 1959 and later purchased the building. The company also manufactured a complete operating table at one time. The business closed in the

Now home to DLH Industries, this building was originally the Knickerbocker Skating Rink. It stands on Kensington Road north of Carrollton, next to the County Highway Garage.

1980s and the building became a Country and Western Restaurant for a short time. Now, the building houses DLH Industries, Inc. which began manufacturing windshield washer lines in 1999. This company is a branch of a Canton business that manufacturers various parts for automobiles.

Gloves were also being manufactured in New Harrisburg at the Eureka Glove Factory. Located in the J.M. Harsh residence, which had formerly been the Elder Store, they made canvas work gloves. The factory operated four machines powered by gas motors in the basement. The little village may not seem like it now, but at that time, it was quite the hub of business. Not only did it house the Eureka Glove Factory, it was also home to a furniture factory, lumbermill, shoemaker, and undertaking establishment. There was also a blacksmith shop, physician, veterinarian, surveyor, several stock dealers, and sign painters.

Another business that started, in 1898, as a foundry was the Ferguson Manufacturing Company. About 1912, it became the Hosterman Novelty Works, which made toys and small metal products. This company was purchased by the George H. Bowman Company, which had been in operation since 1872 and was founded by I.T. Bowman, George's father. George purchased the Hosterman Novelty Works in 1916 and added several new buildings. Soon, this company began manufacturing all sorts of stainless steel products. They were famous for their "Swissalu" brand, which was known nationally. This factory employed 75 men. It later became the Carrollton Metal Products Company, whose first product was aluminum cake savers. During World War II, it was purchased by Walter D. McGruder and his son-in-law Robert H.S. Kaufman, and they turned out several million mess trays for the armed forces. After the war, they were the leader in stainless steel sinks in the United States. In the 1970s, the company was forced to close and the property is now owned by Fusion Ceramics.

A drive through Carroll County makes it apparent that manufacturing is not the main occupation of the residents; it has always been agricultural pursuits. In 1952, Earl Carlton purchased the Robert George farm in Scroggsfield, and in partnership with his wife's uncle John Herbert Graham, they started the Carlton Tree farm. Carlton's three sons, Rick, Ron, and Bruce, also joined the team and continued the business. Every Christmas, some of the finest trees can be found at this farm. Tree farming has become quite a business for Carroll County. Some are strictly for commercial use; others offer trees to the public. Once farming became less profitable, this seemed a likely alternative to all the land available to Carroll County's farmers. There are still many who farm the rolling hills.

Tractors were first used in the area in the 1920s and were mostly made of steel. As they slowly improved and changed to rubber tires, they crowded out the use of horses and mules on many of the farms. Other farm machinery has continued to improve as well, most being labor saving tools.

Augusta Township has always been the major agricultural area, particularly in dairy products. Several early families in the area were of Swiss descent and were quite the cheese makers. A cheese factory was built in the Muddy Fork Valley

This image shows workers at the Eureka Glove Factory in New Harrisburg. (Velma Griffin Collection.)

This artist's rendition shows what the Cummings Bank was to look like before it was built. (Velma Griffin Collection.)

by A. and L. Cunningham. From 1884 to 1886, they made a high grade of Swiss cheese, but discontinued operations in 1886. Nearby, in Minerva, the Minerva Cheese Factory still produces several high-quality cheeses.

Augusta Township was also noted for breeding beef cattle. Before trucks came into use, the cattle would often be herded to market. A. Bryan was a well-known stock buyer who made many trips to Wellsville, so he hired two boys to help drive the cattle. They would be met at Highlandtown by others who would take over from there. The scales to weigh the cattle before their journey began were located in the village of Augusta. Over the years, many 4-H youth have received blue ribbons for their Black Angus, Hereford, and Shorthorn cattle. Other animals have also brought them blue ribbons.

A lot of wool was produced in Augusta Township at one time and most of it was sold in Augusta. Wagonloads would be brought in and the fleece was pitched, one at a time, by a man on the wagon, while a man at the door of the second floor of the Crawford Brothers Store would place it inside.

Fruit and berries have also been grown in Augusta Township. Records show that, in 1893, there were four berry growers and they shipped 600 bushels of strawberries that year. Berries at that time were hauled to Kensington and then shipped to other places by train. The Manfull Orchard is still in operation north of Augusta on Kensington Road. The large strawberry patches that were once

The bank in Sherrodsville is one of the few buildings that remains on Mill Street. (Velma Griffin Collection.)

so dominant are remembered every year at the Augusta Strawberry Festival, sponsored by the Volunteer Fire Department of Augusta Township.

When it comes to food, Carroll County has always had a variety of places to go. The festivals are usually the first choice, but since these are seasonal, the restaurants are a fine second choice. From fine dining places, such as the Atwood Lake Resort, to fast food, there is something for everyone. The first fast-food restaurant in the county was a McDonald's in Minerva, built in the early 1980s, followed by a second in Carrollton in 1987. Now there are several restaurants that fit the fast-food category, including Wendy's, Pizza Hut, Taco Bell, and Subway. The communities throughout Carroll County may no longer be completely self-sufficient in the terms of many businesses, but with easy travel, there is typically a business nearby to fulfill the needs of the citizens.

Of course, with industry came profit and a need to keep these profits safe. Banks entered the scene of the villages almost simultaneously with the coal mines. The earliest record of a bank in Carrollton was in 1870. It was a private banking house, Cummings & Couch, established by James P. Cummings and his brother-in-law Eli Couch. It continued until Couch's death in 1888. It was then simply the Cummings Bank until 1893 when T.J. Saltsman became a partner. In December 1894, it was organized under the state law as a banking company. The name was then the J.P. Cummings Banking Company. The Cummings Bank building was built on the northwest corner of the Public Square and is still a bank today—the National City Bank.

A branch of the Cummings Bank was established in the former Rankin home on Second Street Southwest. It now houses the Veterans Office, Allstate Insurance, and a branch of the National City Bank. The Bank of Magnolia was organized in 1899 by R.E. and C.S. Greer on $20,000 worth of capital. In 1921, the surplus and undivided profits for this institution amounted to $28,000. The brick building that houses the bank was built for $5,000. C.S. Greer sold his half of the interest to Charles E. Beck in 1903, and R.E. Greer and Beck were the sole owners until it was incorporated as a state bank in May 1910. The Bank of Magnolia has expanded to two more locations and is still operating on Main Street in Magnolia.

It was November 4, 1915 when the Minerva Banking Company was organized. The first capital was $25,000, and by 1921, it had doubled. This bank has closed, but Minerva is home to three different banking institution branches, as well as the Minerva Area Federal Credit Union. Likewise, there are five different branches of banking institutions throughout Carroll County.

This image shows High Street in Carrollton. The building to the right was Patterson's Ice Cream shop. At one time, an ice cream factory sat one block south of here. (Courtesy George Rankin.)

9. All Work and No Play . . . Never!

Baseball is probably most associated with the United States, and Carroll County has had its share of teams. The Carrollton team was called the DeLongs. It was organized in 1885 and named for David H. Long, but no one knows for certain why. During the 1888 season, Dent "Cy" Young played for $1 a game. He went on to pitch in the major league and was the only pitcher in the first 100 years of baseball to win 511 games. The DeLongs played anyone they could, mostly teams from the surrounding area, including Canton, East Liverpool, Uhrichsville, Uniontown, and Salineville. According to their score books, they won 71 of the 75 games they played for three seasons. The team folded after the 1890 season and their namesake died in 1891. The team's pitcher, Will M. Coleman, went on to pitch for the Jamestown, New York professional team. After retiring from baseball, he returned to Carrollton where he served two terms as Carroll County Auditor. He was also a deputy in the county treasurer's office and served one term as Carrollton village clerk. The Carrollton team for 1891 was called the Little Giants.

Another member of the former DeLongs was George Hemming, who left Carrollton in 1887 to work at the state mental hospital at Columbus. While playing for the hospital's team, he discovered his pitching ability, and in 1890, was signed to play for the National League in Cleveland. Unfortunately, he only pitched three games that season and was then traded to Brooklyn. He also played for Cincinnati and Louisville. In 1895, he signed with the Baltimore Orioles and pitched for that team when it won the pennant in 1896.

As the prosperity of Carrollton grew, the local hotels became quite popular. The VanHorn House, which was built in 1829 by James Sinclair, was originally a two-story building that housed a mercantile, the second brick building erected in the village. It was purchased in 1867 by Daniel VanHorn, who converted it into a hotel and had the third floor added by John G. Byder. It was considered a first-class hotel in its day, and during the 1890s and early 1900s, enjoyed a large patronage. With a dining room on the second floor, it was capable of seating over 100 guests at a time and was one of the largest in this section of the state. For the convenience

*This photo of Slates Grocery shows the VanHorn House before Daniel VanHorn had the third floor added. (*Centennial Edition.*)*

of travelers, a representative of the hotel would meet guests at the train station. The building is listed on the National Register of Historic Buildings.

The Aldridge Hotel stood just a few feet away from the VanHorn House next to the courthouse. It was later renamed the Park Hotel. After many years of ill repair, it was torn down in the 1990s and the lot became parking for employees of the courthouse.

The Colonial Hotel was only a block away from both the VanHorn House and the Park Hotel. It was built in 1830 by William D. Jenkins and was the third brick structure in the village. On January 1, 1831, before the carpenter had completely finished, the building caught fire and all the woodwork was destroyed. Jenkins commenced rebuilding the next day. Before the charred remains had been completely cleared, he had already begun selling goods in the new building. For several years, the local theater was in this building. It was closed around 1984 and is now the Virginia Lounge.

Now the only hotel in Carrollton is the Days Inn, constructed in 1997. The rooms are designed like suites and it also offers a banquet room and a swimming pool. Prior to its construction, the nearest facility for overnight guests was the Atwood Lake Resort.

The Atwood Lake Resort overlooks the 1,540-acre Atwood Lake and offers 104 rooms, each with a view of the lake. There are also family-type cabins available for rent in the nearby woods. The resort was built along Atwood Lake, which was built as a means of flood control.

Flood control was debated from 1860 to 1913 as it seemed the county was plagued with storms that resulted in flooding. March 1898 saw one of the worst floods known in the history of this area. Carroll County and the surrounding area were badly hit with rains that lasted a week. The gutters in Carrollton were running full; creeks and streams overflowed their banks and spread over everything; towns like Minerva and Malvern were completely underwater; the floor of the depot at Sherrodsville was under 2 feet of running water and the bridge nearby was 3 feet under. Minerva's residents were taken to places of safety in flat boats. Malvern's citizens likened it to a mini-Niagara. Many of the railroad bridges suffered loss. The Oneida Mills bridge was completely destroyed. Four miles of railroad were washed away in Sherrodsville. Harrison County had places that were 9 feet under. Amazingly, there was only one fatality in the entire area, New Hagerstown resident Samuel Hagey. He and his wife had been visiting friends, and on their trip home, the bridge was out. At her insistence, as she wanted to get home to an infant, he tried to cross anyway. The current swept away their buggy, drowning both he and the horse. She was rescued 1 mile downstream by C.V. Clark.

Between March 23 and 27, 1913, two more severe storms caused statewide flooding. This flood took nearly 500 lives and damaged almost $300 million in property. This flood triggered the formation of the Muskingum Watershed Conservancy District (MWCD). Their job was to study the areas along the basin and to establish flood control in the most needed places. Once they completed

The Aldridge Hotel later became the Park Hotel. The building was razed in 1998 and the lot now serves as parking for government employees. (Courtesy of George Rankin.)

their study, the conservancy presented their ideas to Congress. From these studies, the lakes of Atwood, Leesville, and Dover Dam were built.

Letters were sent to the families living in the proposed dam and lake areas, telling them the worth of their properties. Many of these families had lived in the area for several generations and had fought the elements and conquered all that threatened their homes for over 100 years. It was a take-it-or-leave-it situation, and though many held out as long as they could, one by one they gave in and looked for homes elsewhere. While the lakes were being built, squatters moved into the empty homes, only to lose out in 1936 when the waters rose over the dammed creek beds and covered the homesteads and the roads.

Atwood Lake forced the closing of the village of Atwood and the moving of farms, but opened new opportunities by providing jobs during the Depression and saving other farmland and rural communities. It also provided recreational opportunities. The MWCD was also concerned with soil erosion. The project not only practically eliminated flooding and financial loss due to flooding, it brought about reforestation of the area. A floodgate nearly 20 feet high and 60 feet long bridges a gap in the levy at Magnolia. A "necklace" of ten lakes on 709 miles of streams wind their way through the hills of Ohio and include about one-fifth the entire area of the state. Louis Bromfield, Pulitzer Prize winning novelist in 1926 for *Early Autumn*, called it "The Edge of Paradise" when he saw it. Throughout the region are many recreational opportunities: fishing, sailing, camping, hunting, golfing, hiking, picnicking, or simply driving to view the scenery.

Leesville Lake was the first of the lakes to be developed. It was built in 1928 and offers many of the same recreational facilities as Atwood, but is more noteworthy for its many youth and religious camps that surround it. Camp Aldersgate, a ministry of the East Ohio Conference of the United Methodist Church, first leased the land for this camp in 1947 and the first campers attended in 1948. At that time, the camp was a ministry of the Steubenville District of the Methodist church. Later, when the Methodist church and the United Brethren Evangelical Church combined, the camp became a conference site. It is accessed by driving through the Future Farmers of America (FFA) Camp Muskingum on Dyewood Road.

Camp Muskingum is open nearly all year long, offering various learning opportunities to school groups from all over the state of Ohio. Throughout the summer, promising young farmers come to learn new skills and techniques in farming. The facilities are available to the public on a reservation basis. The original buildings at this camp were built in the late 1930s by the National Youth Administration (NYA) to train youth in salable skills. The NYA closed in the early years of World War II and the facilities reverted to the MWCD, who then leased them to the FFA. Their first camp was held in 1944. Over the years, some buildings have been torn down and new areas provided, but several of the original buildings are still in use.

Across the lake from FFA Camp Muskingum is Camp Northeast Ohio Salvation Army (NEOSA), called Camp Twin Spruce in 1973. It is accessed from

This image shows the control tower at Leesville Lake with the dam in the background. (Courtesy Dan Rees.)

the other side of the Lake on Edgewood Road. Further up the lake are Camp Falcon (for boys) built in 1958 and just 1 mile across the lake is Camp Firebird (for girls), which was founded by Marjorie and Bill Lorimer in 1953. Also on Leesville Lake is Camp Wakonda, which is accessed from Leavittsville and is a United Presbyterian Church camp.

In various parts of the county are other camps like Camp Ecco on Pioneer Road, which is operated by the Scio Evangelical Congregation Church. Elkhorn Valley is a Christian Service camp near Bergholz that exists to train Christians to live a Godly life in an ungodly world through weeks of camp and retreats held at the camp or organized through the camp off site. Mechanicstown is home to Camp Gideon Evangelical Friends Camp and Retreat Center.

The Boy Scouts have the Seven Ranges Scout Reservation, southwest of Minerva in Kensington, which encompasses over 900 acres of rolling hills and grassy meadows. While camping, Scouts have the opportunity to use skills they have practiced year round and earn a variety of merit badges. The current ranger for this Buckeye Council camp is Bob Kenyon.

The Girl Scouts also have a camp called the Great Trail Girl Scout Camp, located near Pekin. The Eastern Ohio Basketball camp is located on Dawn Road in Sherrodsville.

Private camping is also offered along Atwood Lake. Campers Paradise and Cozy Ridge Campground are along Fresno Road. Others are The A-1 Twin Valley Campground in Lee Township, Pride Valley Campgrounds in Brown Township, Good's Woods, the Harrison Hills Association, Leesville Southfork Campground, Springhill Campground, and the Maple Valley Campground.

The slogan "The Heart of Vacationland" was adopted in 1961, not only to describe Carroll County, but also to entice city dwellers to visit. A group of three families known as the Carroll Vacationland Association organized to provide an opportunity for city families to spend time on a farm where they could either observe or actually take part in the activities. Cottages and campsites were also available for those who wanted to "rough it." Among the facilities available were Cairn's Bluebird Valley Farm, which is now the Bluebird Gift Shop and Restaurant; Devitt's Seldom Seen Farm; the Twin Valley Campground; Snode's High Hopes Holiday House, now Snode's Melon Farm and Banquet Hall; Haugh's Green Hill Vacation Farm; and Varner's Woodland View Farm.

Private homes also line the shores of Atwood and Leesville Lakes. Another lake that is completely private is Lake Mohawk. It was one of a series of private lakes developed by the American Realty Service Corporation based in Memphis, Tennessee. Lake Mohawk is a 507-acre lake that lies in an 1,800-acre subdivision in Brown and Harrison Townships.

In 1973, a similar area was planned by the same company. It was to be over 2,300 acres with a 300-acre man-made lake. The Countrywood Lake was to sit in Loudon Township, Carroll County and Rumley Township, Harrison County. It would have been the 11th such development in Ohio. The American Realty Service Corporation intended the lake to meet the needs of the outdoor camper, as well as the vacation home site buyer. They intended to offer central water, electricity, comfort stations, recreation areas, and a clubhouse. The site was chosen as it was the site of "Mad" Anthony Wayne's campsite when he traveled through this part of Ohio. This lake never developed.

Vo-Ash Lake, another man-made lake, was built in 1958 by Al Ashbaugh and Charles Voshel of Carrollton for private homes. The overflow portion of the lake was rebuilt in the late 1990s and many homes are still occupied. Not far away, also in Perry Township, is Stony Lake. This is another private lake whose shores are lined with homes and cottages.

Besides camping, the lakes offer many other recreational activities. Boating is available from any one of the marinas, either by renting a boat or docking your own. Swimming is another favorite pastime. For guarded swimming, families can go to the Atwood Lake Park or the Minerva Community Pool during the summer. The Carrollton Vets Club Pool, the Carroll County YMCA, Atwood Resort Lodge, and the Days Inn all offer indoor pools for year-round enjoyment.

There are other recreational activities in the county that do not need water, including bowling with lanes in Carrollton, Minerva, and Dellroy; and exercise through the Carroll County YMCA, Minerva YMCA, or the Aultman Fitness Center. An increasingly popular activity is golfing. Carroll County offers three golf courses. The Atwood Lake Resort has an 18-hole regulation course and a lighted par-3 course. Minerva's Great Trail Golf Course is also an 18-hole course that stradedles the ridge of the Native American and pioneer Great Trail. It is a United States Professional Golfers Association course with lodging and dining. There is also a nine-hole course, a Tee House, and a Pro Shop. In more recent years, the Carroll Meadows was built just north of Carrollton on State Route 39. It is a John Robinson course, offering a full 18 holes. There is a Pro Shop and restaurant called Knickers.

During the summer, the biggest event is the Carroll County Fair. Over 152 years of fairgoers have enjoyed the week-long event. The first fair held was in the original courthouse. According to the commissioner's journal, this was most likely the old Lutheran church on East Main Street where court was held until the courthouse was erected in 1835. The cross hallways through the building were used for exhibiting the samples of wheat, corn, oats, fruit, and other items. The four offices on the first floor were used to display quilts, needlework, bread, cakes, jellies, and things the ladies had to share. Winners in each category did not receive money, but were given certificates, and a few received an article in the form of merchandise presented by local businessmen.

Livestock, such as horses, were exhibited by being hitched to the post-and-rail fences around the public square. The cattle were turned loose in Atkinson's field east of the courthouse, while the sheep and swine were kept in rail pens about where the new courthouse and jail are now located.

Events like horse racing began in 1850 after the Carroll County Agricultural Society was organized. In 1857, 10 acres were leased from Jacob Helfrich for fair purposes. Buildings were then erected on the site for the needed areas. This site was on North Lisbon Street and the racecourse was only a quarter-mile track.

When the lease expired in 1867, it became necessary to find a new site. Seven acres were then purchased from Absalom Aller just north of the Carrollton Corporation line and a tent was erected. Aller still owned 14 acres, and for four days every year, this acreage was rented to the Agricultural Society during the fair. The rest of the year, the acreage was rented out as horse and cow pasture.

In 1880, the society purchased 5 acres of timberland from Isaac Crumrine and had the public road moved to include this acreage. The remaining 14 acres of land owned by Aller were purchased in 1883. The entire fairgrounds were now 26 acres.

Over the years, other improvements were made, such as halls, a grandstand, and stalls and pens for the livestock. Not much changed for several years, then on October 2, 1942, the grandstand caught fire. There were between 1,200 and 1,500 people seated in the stands waiting for the style show and the racing to follow at about 1:30 p.m. Everyone left in an orderly fashion and there were no causalities or injuries, but 20 minutes later, the stand was falling in and was soon burned to the ground. The races were delayed until 3:30 p.m., but were raced as scheduled. It was never completely determined what caused the fire. Approximately 25 concession stands were destroyed. Fire departments from Carrollton, Malvern, Minerva, and Amsterdam responded and were able to keep the fire from spreading beyond the grandstand, but the intense heat prevented saving it. Since World War II was taking place at that time, it was 1949 before materials could be purchased to rebuild the grandstand. This grandstand is still being used today.

The fairgrounds did not see any more major changes until 1966 when 3 acres were purchased from Roy and Pearl Easterday. A year later, lights were installed around the racetrack. Then, in 1971, the society purchased 8 acres from Emil and Mary Ann Pozderac, which was again added to in 1990 when 7 acres were purchased from the Frank Roudebush family. Another year later, an additional two lots were purchased from the Frank Roudebush family, which brings the fairgrounds to a grand total of 44 acres. The highlights of the fair are the music entertainment, 4-H exhibits and auctions, rides, and shows. Thousands of Carroll County citizens, past and present, visit every summer, and as long as farming is strong, so shall be the fair.

In 1895, Leesville had its own fair on October 18, featuring the Bowerston Band and an Anarugeon Parade. Prizes for this fair were given by local merchants and included a parlor lamp for best roll of butter; a pair of overalls for the largest pumpkin; a baby bonnet for the prettiest baby; a free haircut to the man with the longest hair; 50¢ to each person with the largest number of white cats and the cleanest bag of ginseng; and someone offered $50 cash "to the man of my choice at the end of 100 feet of rope." The John Scott Hardware and House Furnishings offered a plug of tobacco to the man with the largest feet.

Possibly the strangest contest was for the ugliest man. Abe Baker the blacksmith won and was given a pocketknife. He was told if he ever met a man uglier, he was to pass the knife on. Several months later, a Mr. Eddleman came to have his team shod and Baker told him there would be no charge and gave him the pocketknife. After Baker told Eddleman why he gave him the knife, Eddleman never came back.

The early Carroll County fairgrounds were on North Lisbon Street. Notice Mr. Helfrich's advertising on the fence. (Courtesy Dick Griffin.)

10. Here and Now

Many changes have come since the first people came to the Carroll County area. The wooded areas are fewer and the villages are bustling with different kinds of activity. Yet, many things still remain the same. When a hand is needed, a neighbor is often quick to help, although they no longer need days of advance notice. Buildings are still being constructed, but now they consist of steel and factory-cut lumber. The homeowner no longer has to clear the land by hand and then cut his own wood.

Our schools are more accessible. Although there are days when a tractor has been seen outside the Carrollton High School, transportation on foot is reserved for students who live close by. The schools are more advanced than just teaching reading, writing, and arithmetic. Today's students, as young as preschool, are becoming computer savvy and there are numerous extracurricular activities that were unheard of in the early 1800s.

Unfortunately, one thing that has not changed is our young men being called to war. Only now, the women join as well and not since the Civil War have the battles come so close to the county. Through two world wars, the Korean War, Vietnam, and Desert Storm, war was something we heard about in the news and cried about as loved ones went off to fight—until September 11, 2001. It is with much sadness that since this book began, the United States has found itself in the midst of yet another fight. On September 11, 2001, the nation was stopped in its tracks when four planes were highjacked, two of which collided with the World Trade Center, one hitting the Pentagon, and another a field in Pennsylvania.

My heart sinks to think that if I had been outside on that very morning, I may have seen Flight 93 as it was turning back over Pennsylvania. According to radar, it indeed flew over the northern portion of our county just minutes before it crashed. Perhaps it was here that Todd Beamer was on the phone with an operator, saying his famous last words: "Let's roll."

In the months that have passed since that day, the changes to Carroll County have been subtle; no longer can our beautiful courthouse be accessed from the front steps. They are chained off and all persons must enter and exit through a door next to the sheriff's office where all belongings are scanned and x-rayed for metal weapons. Families still sit and wait to hear whether a loved one will be returning

This image shows the original grandstand at the Carroll County Fairgrounds. Fairs were originally held in late fall; now they are held in July. (Courtesy Dan Rees.)

from the Middle East or have to go. But we move on, and like all wars before this one, day-to-day life remains the same. We look for all the good we can.

To commemorate the three service units in Carroll County, a flag flown over hostile territory in Afghanistan on a combat mission supporting Operation Enduring Freedom on November 22, 2001 was presented to Howard Drake Jr. and Wayne Davis. It was given to them through Major Robert Michael Koehler, who is a pilot for the U.S. Air Force. A certificate accompanied the flag that was signed by the four members of the KC-135R air refueling air crew, stating that the flag represents recognition of the supreme sacrifice thousands of Americans made during the World Trade Center terrorist attacks.

Similarly, during Desert Storm, a flag that flew over the United States Capitol the day the war started was flown over the square in New Harrisburg. It was given at the request of then congressman Douglas Applegate and raised by John Platt and H.O. Tinlin, who were assisted by a four-man color guard. A special ceremony was held at the square the day the flag was raised. Desert Storm resulted when Iraq refused to withdraw unconditionally from Kuwait.

Other changes to come to Carroll County were made no matter what outside circumstances would have dictated, like the removal of the pine tree from Carrollton's public square. After 15 years of decorating the tree for Christmas, Carrollton's Civic Club decided the tree had become too tall and they were not going to be able to decorate for the 2002 season, one of the reasons being that the lights were about 5 or 6 feet too short! Since the downtown area was being renovated anyway, the Carrollton Council decided it was time for the aged tree to go. It was cut down in the summer and replaced in December with a brand new tree. The old one did not go to waste. It was cut into tree shaped ornaments with the years it stood on the square burned onto them. The ornaments were then sold by the Civic Club.

More renovations were made to the village of Carrollton in 2002, including new sidewalks for the downtown area, new street lights and stop lights, and new street signs. The old street signs had been in place since 1949. Utility lines are now "hidden" underground and new trees line the new sidewalks. Probably the most noticeable change was the removal of the penny parking meters. Many older residents claim the new renovations are reminiscent of days gone by, although many businesses and buildings are gone or changed.

An exciting event taking place is the Bicentennial of Ohio. To commemorate this event, bells were cast in each of the 88 counties. Carroll County's bell was cast at the fairgrounds in July 2002. When Ohio first became a state, there was great need for bells in the schools, courthouses, and churches. Even though bells are no longer as significant in our daily lives, Stephen C. George, executive director of the Bicentennial Commission, hopes the project will guarantee a lasting legacy for the generations that follow. The world's largest bell company, Verdin Company, based in Cincinnati, Ohio, was commissioned to cast the bells. They have been in business since 1842 and created and cast the 33-ton, 12-foot-tall World Peace Bell for the millennium celebration, the "Big Ben" bell in London, and the 1804 San Juan Capastrano Mission Bells.

Carroll County's Bicentennial Bell was on display at the Algonquin Fall Festival.

The company assembled a "foundry on wheels" that made production of the bells a public event. It was a 40-foot, fifth-wheel trailer that carried 12,000 pounds of equipment, including a furnace and sandblaster for bell polishing. The bells were molded in the "American" style of the Liberty Bell and personalized with each county's name, the forging date, the Great Seal of Ohio, and the Bicentennial logo.

The weekend of June 6, 7, and 8, 2003, the Carroll County Historical hosted a Living History Weekend. This included lectures, a train ride, candlelight tour, church service at the Historical Church in Perrysville, a tour of the McCook house, and Civil War reenactments. Many other activities and decorations made this celebration a success.

There are so many more stories of which I am not aware, but are surely equally as fascinating, and I regret that I do not have room for them all. So, I leave you with the words of Peter Herold, who wrote what is possibly the oldest history of Carroll County:

> Now indulgent reader, I have finished my task, as best I could with the data and materials at hand, and with what degree of interest the ANNALS have been received, you alone are to be the judges. I have endeavored to be as fair as the facts would warrant. The statistics that have been used were taken from the official records; and in this connection I desire to acknowledge my indebtedness to [our local officials] and in fact, everyone with whom I came in contact, touching this subject, were ready to furnish such information as was within their knowledge. . . . Yet, it must be conceded that if not altogether faultless, it is the most exhaustive history of the county ever written.

Taken sometime before State Route 183 was established, this dirt road is Main Street Oneida. (Courtesy Dan Rees.)

Bibliography

Books and Articles

Bartley, Roger. "Lost on the Tuscarawas." *A Carroll County Collage.* Jan H. Kennedy, ed. Canton, OH: Zephyr Press, June 1998.

Cavitt, Edward L. "John McTammany, Inventor of the Popular Player Piano." *Carroll County Historical Society Newsletter.* Vol. XVIII, Number 2. (Spring 1989)

Herold, Peter M., ed. *Centennial of Carroll County by Free Press Standard 1815–1915.* Carrollton, OH: The Free Press Standard. 29 July 1915.

Collins, William R. *Ohio: The Buckeye State.* Englewood Cliffs, NJ: Prentice-Hall, Inc., 1956.

Dean, Tanya West and W. David Speas. *Along the Ohio Trail A Short History of Ohio Lands.* Columbus, OH: The Auditor of State Jim Petro, 2001.

Eberhart, G.A. *Historical Atlas of Carroll County Ohio.* Chicago, IL: H.H. Hardesty, 1873.

Eckley, Judge H.J. (Carroll County) and Judge William T. Perry (Harrison County), eds. *History of Carroll and Harrison Counties, OH.* Chicago and New York: Levin Publishing Company, 1921.

Gilson, J.H. *History of the 126th Ohio Volunteer Infantry.* Salem, OH: Walton, Steam Job and Label Printer, 2000.

Griffin, Velma and Lynn R. Fox. *Early History of Carroll County.* Carrollton, OH: Carroll County Historical Society, 1973.

Griffin, Velma. "Belated Historical Recognition." *Ohiana Quarterly.* Vol 15. No. 2 (Summer 1972): 65–69.

———. "New Harrisburg Stagecoach Inn." *Free Press Standard.* 14 March 1968.

"Historical Locations Inventory." New Philadelphia, OH: Tuscarawas Valley Regional Advisory Committee September 1973.

Loomis, Linn. *Here And Now—Ohio's Canals: The Sandy and Beaver Canal.* Sugarcreek, OH: Schlabach Printers, 1994.

Martzolff, Clement L. *Fifty Stories From Ohio History.* Columbus, OH: Ohio Teacher Publishing Company, 1921.

Overman, William D. *Ohio Place Names: The Origin of the Names of over 500 Ohio Cities, Towns and Villages.* Ann Arbor, MI: Edwards Brothers Inc., 1951.

Rutledge, Donald E. "County's role in settling Ohio highlighted as Great Trail Marker is dedicated at Malvern." *Free Press Standard*. 25 April 2002.

———. "Going once - going twice . . . Auctioneer's gavel to fall on New Harrisburg School." *Free Press Standard.* 28 February 1985.

Tope, Margaret E. *Another Little Girl*. Bowerston, OH: The Phrenological Era Print, 1928.

Wallace, Paul A. *Indian Paths of Pennsylvania*. Harrisburg, PA: The Pennsylvania Historical and Museum Commission, 1965.

Wilder, Howard B., Robert P. Ludlum, and Harriet McCune Brown. *This is America's Story*. Cambridge, MA: Houghton Mifflin Co., 1954.

Zwick, Bette O. "Carroll County Courthouse." *A Carroll County Collage.* Jan H. Kennedy, ed. Canton, OH: Zephyr Press, June 1998.

Directories and Miscellaneous

Baer, Pat and Virginia Nash. "A History of Leesville, Ohio." Unpublished manuscript, 2 July 1976.

Conway, Emmett A. Sr. "The Great Trail" at http://www.users.hockinghills.net.

Farragut, David. "Untitled Autobiography." Unpublished manuscript, New York Public Library.

Gray, Karen Jones. "History of Education in the Dellroy Area." Unpublished manuscript, 2 August 1978.

"History of Kilgore." Unpublished manuscript.

Markley, Thomas G. "Indian Lore." Unpublished manuscript.

Morgan's Men Association. http://members.tripod.com/~Morgans.men/

Nash, Virginia. "Legends of the Conotton Valley." Unpublished manuscript.

Schandel, Irene Armstrong. "The Homeland." Unpublished manuscript.

Sherrodsville Elementary Third and Sixth grades. "The Sherrodsville Standard: A History of Sherrodsville." 4 June 1998.

Woodward, Taylor C. "History of Augusta Township." Unpublished manuscript.

Newspapers

Carroll Chronicle. September 1898.

Carroll Journal. 1880, 1938-1943.

The Elderberry Special. June 2002.

INDEX

Appleseed, Johnny, 7, 10, 11, 21
Atkinson, Isaac, 32, 46, 47, 48
Bohart, Peter, 32–33, 46, 47, 96
Craig, Isaac, 30, 31, 32, 35
Desert Storm, 153, 154
Downing, James, 11–12, 28, 34
Elderberry Line, 53–54. 56. 57. 63
Fighting McCooks, 7, 47, 48, 74, 89, 117–122, 138
The Great Trail, 9, 10, 11, 13, 14, 16, 24, 149, 150
Kangaroo Crossing, 52
Lee, Alexander, 28
McCook, Daniel, 47, 48, 117–118, 122
Miller, Isaac, 11, 12, 28, 41
Native Americans, 7, 8, 9, 13, 14, 16, 19, 26, 97, 119, 150
Captain Pipe, 11, 16, 19
Chief White Eyes, 19–20
Ohi-Rail, 57, 63, 64
Operation Enduring Freedom, 154
Palmer, Jesse, 25, 26
Pigtown, 129
Revolutionary War, 15, 19, 32, 35, 97
Sandy-Beaver Canal, 41–44, 50, 53
Seven Ranges, 15, 16, 17, 149
Sherrod, William, 26, 27
Temperance Movement, 128
Townships
  Brown, 30, 34, 35, 36, 41, 46, 53, 59, 71, 73, 93, 149, 150
  East, 45, 46, 78, 124
  Fox, 24, 46, 84, 85, 116, 123, 124, 125
  Lee, 25, 44, 46, 73, 79, 105, 108, 122, 127, 149
  Loudon, 16, 26, 46, 94, 150
  Monroe, 26, 27, 29, 30, 46, 52, 81, 112
Vail, Theodore Newton, 71, 72
Villages
  Atwood, 20, 37, 38, 82, 148
  Augusta, 13, 24, 33, 46, 57, 58, 59, 64, 66, 67, 70, 72, 73, 76, 78, 97, 99, 101, 102, 106, 115, 122, 123, 127, 130, 141–143
  Carrollton, 2, 8, 12, 13, 20, 27, 28, 32, 36, 45, 46, 47, 51–57, 59, 65–69, 71, 75–81, 83–84, 86–92, 95, 96, 101–105, 108, 111, 113–117, 122, 124, 126, 129–132, 136–140, 143, 145–147, 150, 151, 153–155
  Centreville, 33, 46, 47, 67, 87, 89, 95, 96, 109
  Dellroy, 11, 21, 29, 30, 52, 54–56, 65, 80–82, 108–112, 115, 150
  Downingville, 28
  Harlem Springs, 10, 25, 28, 44, 45, 67, 68, 79, 80, 87–89, 95, 102, 103, 105–107, 109, 123
  Hibbets, 56, 59, 60, 61
  Kilgore, 16, 25, 26, 50, 61, 80, 95, 101, 109, 115, 126

Leavittsville, 30, 52, 85, 100, 109, 128, 138, 149
Leesville, 27, 28, 63, 65, 67, 85, 109, 115, 124–126, 128, 129, 136, 137, 148–150, 152
Magnolia, 9, 28, 42, 51, 56, 83, 112, 144, 148
Malvern, 9, 14, 31, 36, 41–43, 53, 66–68, 71, 72, 74, 87, 93, 103, 106, 111, 115, 128, 132, 133, 147, 151
Mechanicstown, 51, 52, 63, 78, 84, 85, 101, 149
Millensburgh, 28, 103, 107
Minerva, 9, 11, 35, 36, 41, 42, 50, 53–59, 63, 64, 66, 67, 75, 77, 87, 142, 143, 144, 147, 149, 150, 151
Norristown, 45, 87, 123
Oneida, 9, 30, 31, 35, 36, 42, 43, 53–56, 68, 103, 147
Pattersonville, 52, 58, 63, 66, 70, 73, 77, 101, 102, 127
Pekin, 9, 14, 30, 31, 32, 35, 41, 44, 53, 64, 67, 94, 149
Perrysville, 50, 51, 65, 69, 71, 82, 102, 109, 110, 117, 119, 120, 156
Petersburg, 37, 66, 84, 109
Queensboro, 27
Sherrodsville, 27, 28, 55, 56, 68, 71, 85, 99, 109, 112, 115, 132, 147, 149
Specht, 58, 63, 128, 139
War of 1812, 33, 35, 94
Wathey's Station, 58
Wheeling and Lake Erie Railroad, 133
Wiggins, Isaac, 44, 45, 102, 105, 107

The Carrollton Nine, as they were called, were the Carrollton High School Baseball team. (Courtesy Dan Rees.)